HIDDEN
IN PLAIN SIGHT

HIDDEN
IN PLAIN SIGHT

The Secret of More

MARK
BUCHANAN

Published by
THOMAS NELSON™
Since 1798

Published in Nashville, Tennesse by Thomas Nelson, Inc.

Published in association with the literary agency of Ann Spangler and Company, 1420 Pontiac Road SE, Grand Rapids, MI 49506.

All Scripture quotations, unless otherwise indicated, are taken from The Holy Bible, New International Version. Copyright © 1973, 1978, 1984, International Bible Society. Used by permission of Zondervan Bible Publishers.

Scripture quotations marked (NKJV) are taken from The New King James Version, copyright © 1979, 1980, 1982, Thomas Nelson, Inc., Publishers.

Editorial Staff: Greg Daniel, acquisitions editor, and Thom Chittom, managing editor.
Cover Design: John Hamilton
Page Design: Walter Petrie

ISBN-13: 978-0-8499-0174-4

To Carol Patricia Boschma,
(March 8, 1965–August 8, 2006)

whose love for the Father's house
helped us all come to our senses
and long to come home.

If anyone chooses to do God's will, he will find out whether my teaching comes from God or whether I speak on my own.

JOHN 7:17

We shall not cease from exploration
And the end of our exploring
Will be to arrive where we started
And know the place for the first time.

T. S. ELIOT
"Little Gidding"
V, stanzas 239–242
The Four Quartets

Contents

II. Make Every Effort

III. Reap a Harvest

Preface

Come in Here with Me

I WENT SPELUNKING LAST SUMMER WITH MY DAUGHTER NICOLA, nine years old at the time, and forty of her classmates. Spelunking is cave exploring. Spelunking means you find some pleat in the earth's crust and slither, lizard-like, into it. You thread your way down shafts narrow as the grave, shimmy your way up holes tight as chimney flues. You emerge into vaults and caverns hidden forever from sun and wind, hewn by the brute violence of tectonics, the solemn patience of melting ice, the slow burnish of trickling water.

I didn't think I'd be up for it. I suffer mild claustrophobia and can easily relive the terror of a childhood event in which my brother and his friend locked me in a trailer's closet. I panicked. I rammed my shoulder against the thin mahogany door, splintered it off its hinges. The trailer belonged to the parents of my brother's friend, and he stood to catch trouble for the damage. I couldn't have cared less.

So spelunking held no initial charm. To enter one cave I had to flatten my body to a knife blade, insert it between a thin cleft of rock, and step into the underworld's thick silence and thicker darkness. I picked my way down a staircase of boulders. I descended twisting chutes, squeezed between narrowing shafts, shoehorned myself through rock eyelets, duckwalked damp tunnels. The trail led nowhere, just further in, deeper down.

Why did I come?

It was unclear at first. I came to test something, to prove something, to overcome something. I came to see things daylight can't produce. I came because it's shameful to fear the dark at my age. I came because my daughter and her classmates needed me in some vague, loose way, and I couldn't let them down. Nor let them show me up.

And what did I discover?

Beauty beyond imagining. Stalactites long and sharp as Zeus' thunderbolts. Stalagmites tall and jagged as tiger-pit stakes. Snowy-white cascades of calcite. Filigrees of encrusted mineral. Exotic rock sculptures finessed by seepage, as though by fingertips, over eons. And then, when all the flashlights turned out, a blackness so complete it is one of the few holy and perfect things I've touched in this unholy, imperfect world.

THIS IS A BOOK ABOUT PRACTICING VIRTUE, WHICH AT FIRST may seem—it did to me—a descent into something narrow and dark and enclosing, a world without wind, without open spaces where weather dances its varied moods. The word *virtue* almost made me claustrophobic. By temperament and against better instinct, I still have moments where I think the good life is seeking my own pleasure at my own convenience, and so the very thought of practicing virtue chafed me. I pictured Victorian women bound in corsets. I pictured Mormon boys in starched white shirts and crisp ties, earnestly soliciting at my door. I pictured primness and stiffness and pursed lips and arched eyebrows.

I never imagined life to the full.

But that's what I'm discovering: a world vast and beautiful and holy—that all along has been hidden in plain sight.

Why don't you come in here with me, and see for yourself?

Introduction

The Incredible Shrinking Man

IN CHILDHOOD I WAS OFTEN AND UNPREDICTABLY STRUCK WITH an odd sensation: I felt I was shrinking. The feeling was as sudden and startling (though more pleasant) as skinning my knee in a fall, as abrupt as plunging naked into cold water. The only necessary condition was that I had to be still. Otherwise it could hit me day or night, half-asleep or wide awake, upright or prone. I'd be standing beside a field at day's end, sunlight serrating the edges of thunderheads, watching my friends in a clumsy game of softball. Or I'd be slumped on the couch at midday, reading a *Spiderman* comic, bored and transfixed by its gaudy spectacle. Or I'd be curled up on my bed at night, sinking fast into sleep's netherworld.

And then it might hit me, or not, this odd sensation of shrinking. I experienced it as an actual coiling and compacting in my limbs. It spread from there to my midriff and head. It was as though my body's molecules, one minute turning lazy arcs in wide circles, moved together, quick and steady, until they had no room to move at all. My body became heavy as water, tight as a fist.

And then I had another sensation: of looking out from my body, now miniscule, on a world grown preposterously large. Trees and

1

pets and lamps and furniture had swollen to gargantuan proportions. The world towered and loomed, gaped and sprawled. I was Gulliver among giants.

And then it would be over. The entire experience lasted, I'm guessing, ten seconds at most. Probably less. I couldn't conjure it, though sometimes I tried. I neither welcomed it nor shunned it. I didn't understand it, and still don't. It was just something that happened to me, a vestige of instinct, a quirk of genes, a glitch of biorhythms. I assumed it happened to everyone. I outgrew it in early adulthood, though it's happened once or twice since.

There must be some neurological explanation for what I'm describing. There might even be a condition here, a viral trace, a syndrome of sorts. Until I started writing this, it never occurred to me to check any of that. I simply wanted to tell you about my childhood experience—even at the risk of appearing freakish in your eyes—because, since late adulthood, I have been trying to produce its spiritual equivalent: to become small, small, ever smaller, reduced to my core, as the world grows big, big, ever bigger, expanded to its limits. I want to decrease, and Christ and his kingdom to increase.

I'm having limited success.

This is the fifth book. All of them are different, and all of them the same. They're the same at this single juncture: Each is preoccupied with the question, *How do I get more of God in my life?* What combination of discipline and serendipity, striving and resting, what mix of painstaking study, freewheeling worship, wildfaring play is needed if I'm to decrease and Christ is to increase? Where must I die to myself, and where become more alive? What needs throttling, what invigorating? Which branches ought I to prune ruthlessly, and which to graft tenderly?

Five books now. One on spiritual formation, one on heavenly

mindedness, one on God's character, one on rediscovering Sabbath. They've ranged over a wide field. But, always, this singular obsession: *Is there more?*

Now this book. It's different again—a book on virtue. Yet it returns, with migratory hunger, to that question that haunts and hounds me, binds and looses me, that question that either I can't let go of or that won't let go of me. *Is there more?*

Yes.

The answer's been hidden in plain sight for almost two thousand years, so underfoot we deemed it not worth picking up, like a rare coin we mistook for a penny. In this case, the coin is a mere seven verses, and the ground it lies upon a seldom-cited book by a man named Peter, a wind-chastened fisherman turned pastor. Peter lived three years shoulder-to-shoulder with Jesus, in the rough-and-tumble of a friendship that left him changed ever after. Out of that experience he wrote two letters. In the second one, right at its beginning, he tells us about seven old things to make life new.

That's our coin, the secret of more.

This book is about those seven things.

THE NEXT ELEVEN CHAPTERS COMPRISE THE HEART OF THIS book: an introductory chapter, two chapters on the nature of faith, one on the role of the Spirit, and seven chapters on virtue, at least the seven virtues Peter commends.

But as I wrote, I became curious about Peter the man. I'm a pastor, and I've discovered my greatest occupational hazard is speaking of things I know nothing about. I have a friend, also a pastor, who calls it "trafficking in unfelt truth"—commending to others a life we've never lived, posing as tour guides to territory on which we've never set foot. It's a spiritual discipline all on its own just to steer clear of that hazard.

I have also discovered another thing: God has a way of engineering circumstances to throw a pastor head-first into whatever he presumes to teach. So when I teach on controlling anger, I typically have a week that severely tests my serenity, full of breakages and upheavals. When I speak on overcoming temptation, usually some enticement sidles up close, and the ground gets slippery beneath me. When I preach on prayer, often I am inundated under a landslide of interruptions that could easily render me prayerless.

So I became curious about Peter. He wrote about seven virtues. How did he himself exhibit them? Struggle with them? Learn obedience in practicing them through his suffering? How did God take a man who, when we first meet him, showed little signs of possessing these seven traits, and not only inspire him to write an epistle about them, but apprentice him until he became a living epistle for them?

That curiosity took shape in a series of short reflections that, collectively, I've called the *Petrine Diaries*—Petrine is the adjectival form of Peter. I've written eleven of these in all, one to follow each of the main chapters. And then, as a kind of final tribute, I've written two closing chapters that recount the lessons Peter has taught me in my year of traveling with him.

ONE LAST THING BEFORE WE START. I BEGAN AS A FICTION writer, and soon I intend to return to that. So here I've indulged myself a little and written three short stories. I've placed one at the end of each section of this book.

These stories are about Peter from the perspective of someone who knew him—James, his fishing partner; Peter's unnamed wife;

and Andrew, his brother. They are works of imagination, not theology, meant to do no more than to stir up your imagination.

Which, come to think of it, may just be what theology is and does too.

IN THE MOVIE *SECONDHAND LIONS*, TWO OLD CURMUDGEONS, Hub and Garth, assume the care of Hub's ten-year-old nephew, Walter, after his mother abandons him. The two men are at first reluctant hosts, especially Uncle Hub. He begrudges Walter the little food he eats, the small space he takes up. The two old men live in a dilapidated farmhouse, the fields roundabout gone to seed, and spend most days sitting on their tumbledown porch, shotguns straddling their laps, nursing a giant grudge against the world, and taking potshots at any traveling salesmen foolhardy enough to venture near. They want to be left alone, to die quietly in their misery.

They don't care about nothin'.

But the boy's presence works a miracle: their withered hearts grow young again, learn to love again. They start to hunger for more. They start spending their enormous fortune—they possess, mysteriously, a cache of money hidden somewhere on their land—on everything from garden seeds and garden tools, to a catapult that flings plates skyward for shooting practice, to a Red Baron–style airplane, to a secondhand lion, a mangy old feline who just wants, like they did, to finish her days in undisturbed idleness.

As the old men's hearts awaken, they tell Walter, slowly, their story. Uncle Hub was once a swashbuckling adventurer, a poet-warrior, and Garth his trusted sidekick. Together, they lived an enchanted, dangerous life, routing armies, plundering treasures, rescuing a damsel in distress. Together, they outwitted a cunning and noble enemy, an

Arabian sheik, Uncle Hub's rival for the love of his beautiful Jasmine.

Walter is never sure whether to believe these stories. He wants to, but they're so outsized and exotic, and these arthritic cranky old men, even as they wake, bear little resemblance to the legendary heroes they describe in their stories.

But to tell the stories is to re-inhabit them. Those two old men, in their closing years, become every bit as headlong and two-fisted as they claimed to be in their youth. They finish well. They die in their nineties, full of days, joyriding their plane with such reckless abandon they crash it upside down into the barn door. They punch that door so clean and hard they cookie cut a hole, perfectly plane-shaped, right through it.

Walter, now grown, comes to survey the scene of their death. As he stands outside the house, a helicopter rises over the trees and comes down beside him. A handsome young man, around his age, steps out. He is dark-skinned, middle-eastern. Walter realizes it's the grandson of Hub's legendary rival, the sheik. Both men grew up hearing fantastic tales of sword fights and narrow escapes and buried treasures, and both wondered if the tales were true. The Sheik's son looks at everything, the farm, the barn, the hole where the plane hit.

"So," he says, astonished, "it's true after all. They really lived."

Walter smiles.

"Yes," he says. "They *really* lived."

That's my hope for this book. May it disrupt us, turn us upside down in order to live right-side up. May it help us live lives worthy of our calling, neither hoarding nor grudging but gladly spending and being spent for the kingdom of God.

May it help us live with such holy vigor that when we're gone, our epitaph will be "They *really* lived."

I

Prepare the Ground

1

I Want More

I WATCHED A THIN BLADE OF MOONLIGHT MIGRATE ACROSS THE room. I searched for pockets of coolness among the sheets. I listened to night sounds: the hoots and whirrs and shrills of nocturnal things, the elegiac groaning of timber contracting in the gathering chillness.

I'd had close to six months to prepare for this, and still I felt unprepared. I couldn't sleep. I went over it again, and again, and then again, in my mind: I would open with a question, let it linger on the air briefly, then read the Bible passage. I would pause dramatically in two places, as though struck fresh with revelation. And then I'd launch into the story, one of my crackerjacks. I'd tell it in a way that would ratchet up the tension. And then, when the whole thing was taut to breaking, trembling with the strain, I'd resolve it cleanly with a conclusion both surprising and obvious, the kind you should have seen all along.

In the morning, I had to preach—for five minutes. I do a lot of public speaking. I usually feel no more anxiety about it than I do swimming. But this was different: this was preaching to my peers, twenty-six of them. We were halfway through a two-year leadership course, and the day had come when we had to showcase our homiletic skills for one another. Not one among us, I think, relished that duty. We were all nervous with wanting to impress one another. With wanting to be better than one another. At least I was.

Morning came, and we assembled. The instructor had assigned us our places in the lineup. I was seventeenth. We began. My peers were good. Intimidatingly so. Witty, earnest, heartfelt, balancing with acrobatic agility, substance with showmanship. When my turn came, my confidence was bruised, but I did all right. Everyone said so.

Steve was, I think, number twenty-two. Unlike most of us, he was not a seasoned speaker, not back then, anyhow. Preaching wasn't his day job. He walked up to the front, and we could see he was shaking. When he turned around, his eyes were wide with fear. "I'm scared," he said.

"It's okay, Steve," we said. "It's just us."

Steve told the story from Luke's Gospel, about the woman who was bleeding for twelve years and who, bankrupt from medical bills, ready to give up, threaded her way through a teeming crowd to touch the hem of Jesus's robe. She managed that, then melted away into the crowd. But Jesus knew. He stopped—even though he was in a hurry, trying to get to Jairus' house before his daughter succumbed to her illness—and drew the woman out. That one touch, deliberate, desperate, faith-filled, did what years of doctors' nostrums and platitudes failed to do: healed her.

Steve told the story, no embellishments, no dramatic flair. He might just have read it. Still, when he finished, we were silent. Something holy had taken place. We were, at the very least, caught up in the wonder of that long-ago moment, that fearful, hopeful woman touching Jesus and walking away with health brimming in every part of her. Twelve years of bleeding, all the mess and cost and stench and weariness of it, gone in an instant.

We were supposed to critique one another, but no one wanted to do this with Steve. We sat in stone stillness. In the room's quietness, we heard weeping. We all turned, and saw that it was Wendy, the administrator. She had been taping our speeches, but now she sat catching tears in her hands. The instructor asked if she was okay. "Yes," she said. "Yes."

She calmed herself, and then told us what had happened.

"For four months, I have been in constant pain. I have been to my doctor several times. She sent me to see specialists. They ordered test after test. None could tell me what's wrong. My husband and I have been frustrated and afraid. We told no one. I thought I'd have to live with this the rest of my life."

Wendy started to weep again.

"But when Steve started to speak, Jesus came and healed me."

We applauded. We congratulated Wendy. We congratulated Steve. We thanked God.

But I also sat there ashamed. I had been so anxious to impress everyone else, to best everyone else, there was no room left in my striving for Jesus. It took Steve, in weakness, in fear and trembling, for God to come in power.

That night, I couldn't sleep again. This time, though, it was a different thought that kept me awake: *I want more, God. I want more of you.*

And I think he said, *I want that for you, too.*

ON JANUARY 8, 1918, U.S. PRESIDENT WOODROW WILSON MADE a speech to Congress. The U.S. had entered the continental war—

later known as WWI—nine months earlier, though that conflict had engulfed Europe in blood and fire for more than three years, and wouldn't end for almost another year. Wilson delivered the so-called Fourteen Points address: an enumeration of America's political postwar aims. These were clear, concrete, and specific objectives—the fair settlement of territories, the restoration of borders, the protection or relocation of ethnic groups, and the like. Wilson outlined, with sober precision, the key tasks to be accomplished. There was not a bit of pulpit bluster or rhetorical vagueness in anything he said.

Almost twenty-three years to the day—January 6, 1941—U.S. President Franklin Delano Roosevelt made a speech to Congress. This was a mere seven months after the eruption of WWII in Europe, when America was still debating the scope and nature of its role in that conflict. Roosevelt delivered the so-called Four Freedoms address: an elucidation of America's cultural aims upon entering the war.

Roosevelt's speech was markedly different in content, purpose, and tone from Wilson's. Where Wilson had, item by item, sketched out geopolitical objectives that both justified and defined America's overseas involvement, Roosevelt cast a vision as wide as earth and high as heaven. He spoke, stirringly, passionately, poetically, of four liberties that, together, comprised humanity's birthright: freedom of speech, freedom of worship, freedom from want, and freedom from fear. To this end, for this cause, America must fight.[1]

Wilson's speech was short on vision and long on details, Roosevelt's the opposite. Wilson was pragmatic, but uninspiring; Roosevelt charismatic, but vague. The first advised, the second aroused. The one directed policy and the other ignited imaginations. One told us what to do, and the other why we ought to do it.

Wilson's speech was a call to take up hammer and plow, Roosevelt's, sword and banner.

I love the Bible for many reasons, but one is that it does both these things, often at once: awakens the imagination, and informs the mind; stirs souls, and directs paths; captures the heart, and then instructs it. It's also why I cherish the work of the Holy Spirit within me: the Spirit sweeps me up in wild exhilaration, and then, step by almost plodding step, leads me into all truth, teaching me, reminding me, lighting my path as I go.

This book explores a single biblical passage that works this way. It is as practical as Wilson's "Fourteen Points" and inspiring as Roosevelt's "Four Freedoms." The passage is from a biblical letter that is seldom cited, little read, and rarely preached. This is all too bad, and to our loss.

For it is stunning in its combination of utmost simplicity and utter audacity. It promises the whole world, and more besides. It inspires and instructs all at once, and reveals the secret of *more*— more purpose, more passion, more life.

More of God.

Here it is:

Simon Peter, a servant and apostle of Jesus Christ,

To those who through the righteousness of our God and Savior Jesus Christ have received a faith as precious as ours:

Grace and peace be yours in abundance through the knowledge of God and of Jesus our Lord.

His divine power has given us everything we need for life and godliness through our knowledge of him who called us by his own glory and goodness. Through these he has given us his very great and precious promises, so that through them you may participate in the divine nature and escape the corruption in the world caused by evil desires.

For this very reason, make every effort to add to your faith goodness; and to goodness, knowledge; and to knowledge, self-control; and to self-control, perseverance; and to perseverance, godliness; and to godliness, brotherly kindness; and to brotherly kindness, love. For if you possess these qualities in increasing measure, they will keep you from being ineffective and unproductive in your knowledge of our Lord Jesus Christ. But if anyone does not have them, he's nearsighted and blind, and has forgotten that he has been cleansed from his past sins. (2 Pet. 1:1–9)

Everything you need for life and godliness you have already. In full. You actually don't need any *more*. Not one thing—not a cotter pin or flat washer, not a doohicky or a thingamajig: nothing's been withheld. Everything required for *zoë*—abundant and flourishing life—and *eusebeia*—a deep and real commitment to what matters most—is intact.

The life you've always wanted is already here. Right now. Not next year. Not after you get through this particularly difficult season. Not after your kids reach a certain age. Not after your husband gets his act together, or you've gone to counseling, or acquired a college degree, or read the latest and greatest self-help book.

Here and now you have everything you need.

Only, there's some assembly required. Peter says, "For this very reason"—because you have all you need, down to the last snip of thread and patch of duct tape—"*for this very reason*, make every effort to add . . ."

What follows are seven virtues, each and all laid on the foundation of faith. Seven virtues that we're to make every effort to acquire. And if we do? We will participate in God's very own nature. We will escape the corruption of the world. We will lead a fruitful and productive life.

We will have more.

It's that simple.

BUT MAYBE YOU'RE CYNICAL ABOUT THIS.

The years often diminish us. No matter how we wish it otherwise, how hard we try and pray and regret and resolve, we often find ourselves with less, not more. Elsewhere, I've called this condition borderland, where the life we live only parodies the dreams we've dreamed.[2]

So many things hold us back or set us back. Old wounds. Old fears. Old ways. There's *that* man who always pushes *that* button, and though you've told yourself a thousand times that it won't happen this time, it does. There's that sin that you've repented of beyond counting—you've gone to the altar, you've gone to the cross, you've gone to the counselor, you've gone half insane, and still it plagues you, and mocks you, and gloats over you, and makes you its minion and plaything.

The pastor who prays like Elijah, preaches like Spurgeon, counsels like Nouwen, and who late at night slips out of bed, his wife soundly sleeping, and lusts like Caligula, devouring Internet porn. He returns to bed, numb and glutted, and tells himself that's it, that's the end of it. It never is.

The wife and mother who savors every moment of her early mornings, soaking in Scripture, pouring out prayer, but whose temper is an unstable fault line: the least little thing—spilled juice, the muffins burning, the children asking something at the wrong time—

can twist it open, and the whole house shakes. She's apologized to her son so many times that now he gives her a wary, bitter look and is starting to stutter, and he's only five.

The young lady just starting college, who signed up the first day to help with a campus ministry because, as she says, "I just love Jesus and want to serve him however I can," but who keeps inviting guys over to her dorm, and always things go further than she intended. She wonders what it is about her that she can't say no.

The elder who speaks with heartfelt conviction—you thought he was going to cry last Sunday when he prayed—about God's love for everyone, but who secretly resents the Asians attending his church and wonders why they don't find "a fellowship more suited to their own kind."

Something chases most of us. Some dark appetite, some deep prejudice, some wildcard emotion. We usually find ways to manage it: stitch fig leaves to conceal it, develop verbal ruses to deny it, borrow pat explanations to justify it. But we feel its stain and weight. We know it offends a holy God. And we wish he'd just show up in our sleep and pluck the thing clean out, and let us wake up as wholly new creations.

The years pass, and instead we make our home with our sins and our demons, and just hope no one finds out.

THE EARLY CHURCH GAVE SPECIFIC NAMES TO OUR CHRONIC plight. They called them the Seven Deadly Sins: pride, envy, greed, sloth, gluttony, anger, lust. Each is not just a sin in itself, but also a root of sinfulness: a sin that *causes* sin. Greed, for example. That's a sin all by itself. But it's also the seed of thievery, hoarding, lying, exploitation, injustice, addiction—a breeding ground for a host of evildoing.

A fourth-century ascetic named Evagrius of Pontus, rawboned and austere, cobbled together hints from earlier monk-theologians and came up with the idea that there existed, underneath particular acts of sin, some deadly ones, the real poison in the well. He numbered them at eight. Two centuries later, Pope Gregory shaved these to seven. In the twelfth century, Thomas Aquinas took the idea and popularized it, and in the sixteenth century, Sir Edmund Spenser and then Dante took the idea and immortalized it. In Spenser's whimsical, colorful, often lurid poem *The Faerie Queen*, he depicts the Seven Deadly Sins rattling through town in noisy gaudy pageant: Pride in a royal carriage pulled by a menagerie of beasts, each mounted by one of the other six sins.[3] Gluttony, his belly "up-blowne with luxury," rides a "filthie swine" and gorges himself as he goes, gulping continuously from a "bouzing can" (sec. 21–23). Lechery, or Lust, parades upon a he-goat, lewd and charming all at once, loaded with cheap enticements. "He well could daunce, and sing with ruefulnesse,/ And fortunes tell, and read in loving bookes,/ And thousand other wayes, to bait his fleshly hooks" (sec. 24–26). Avarice, mounted on a camel to tote his iron coffers stuffed with gold, is gaunt and sharp-eyed, laden with wealth yet dressed in rags and festering with open sores (sec. 27–29). All Seven Sins act in kind.

Dante, for his part, imagined hell's architecture comprised of seven levels, each corresponding to one of the Seven Sins, with punishment meted out at each level to match the crime.

Ever since, to varying degrees the concept of the Seven Deadly Sins has provided a clear explanation for the trouble we're in, from wars and genocides to wife abuse and check fraud, from white lies to bloody Sundays, from haughty looks to holocausts.

The concept is not, strictly speaking, biblical. Of course, the

Bible is candid about the problem of sin. Paul, David, Jesus, Moses, Isaiah—none was soft on sin nor vague about it. They named it outright, without euphemism or hedging, warned of its wiles and traps. Yet none of them ever mentions Seven Deadly Sins—they saw all sin and all sinfulness as deadly, its wages paid in the hard cold coin of death. The Bible contains sin lists (Proverbs, Paul's letters), but gives no precise enumeration. Indeed, the lists appear partial, representative, evocative.

Still, the idea that there are some sins that breed sins is deeply biblical. Jesus said to be worried, not so much about the things that come into the body—a mouthful of bread, a throatful of wine, a bellyful of pie—but about the things that come out of the heart—greed, jealousy, lust, and the like. When Paul knocks off a sin list, many of them seem more root than fruit—sins that generate sins. Envy, rage, slander. These are sins all by themselves. But each is also a hothouse of vice that unstopped can ruin a household, a church, a nation. James approaches something close to the idea of sin-causing sins when he describes the tongue:

> Consider what a great forest is set on fire by a small spark. The tongue also is a fire, a world of evil among the parts of the body. It corrupts the whole person, sets the whole course of his life on fire, and is itself set on fire by hell. (James 3:5b–6)

The concept of Seven Deadly Sins cannot be grounded in chapter and verse of Scripture, but it stems from a solid biblical base.

And they are with us always, these deadly sins. We never arrive at a place where they no longer hold sway or pose threat. Daily, they require our vigilance. Lifelong, they call for our diligence. You crush the head of one, another slithers out some crack in the wall.

So we're always fighting a trench war, bruised and weary, just holding off the onslaught.

But we want more.

Does God want more for us?

He does, and hid it in plain sight. All along he's given us seven old things, seven virtues, to make life new. And all we have to do is find them.

THE BIBLE TELLS THE STORY OF THE TROUBLE WE'RE IN, BUT ITS greater story is about the grace we've received. It recounts what God's done, and still does, to get us out of trouble, a breathtakingly dramatic tale of a lover who lost his bride and went to extravagant, heroic, even foolhardy lengths to win her back: a long and perilous journey, a grim and bloody battle, a seemingly disastrous ending, an unexpected and astonishing reversal. And it is the story of the lover's intent, not just to rescue her from the dragon and his lair, but to bring her to his castle and make her spotless, radiant, unblemished.

God has no less an ambition than to take people captive to evil and ruined by sin and to transform them, while yet on earth, into the likeness of Jesus. The transformation is not completed until heaven, but God wants to get it well under way on this side.

The Spirit of Jesus, the one who rescued us, lives in those who embrace him. By his Spirit, we are made new. But that Spirit does not work out of thin air or motivate us with hot air. He does not conjure newness and wholeness out of mere wishful thinking or stern lecturing. God is a God of means, and the chief means he uses are disciplines we embrace and practice. We walk a path of fellowship and worship, humility and attentiveness. We soak ourselves in the Word, ground ourselves in prayer, place ourselves in community. The Spirit takes these things, meager as they are, and works miracles from them. He receives our few loaves and fishes, and multiplies them a thousandfold.

But first we bring our loaves and fishes.

This book is about bringing those loaves and fishes—seven, to be exact. It's about seven God-given disciplines we undertake so the Spirit can multiply our small effort into more than we can ask or imagine. It's about seven seeds we plant and cultivate so the Spirit can bear much fruit in us and through us. It's about seven gifts the bride brings to her dowry, and then the bridegroom uses to perfect her.

It's about seven virtues.

One of my underlying assumptions about these seven virtues is that each, just as with the Seven Deadly Sins, are not just virtues all by themselves but also seedbeds of goodness. They generate virtuousness. So, for example, brotherly kindness. This is a good trait all on its own. But it has the power to produce forgiveness, repentance, humility, unity, trustworthiness. It builds community, enriches friendship, inspires servanthood. It overturns, among other vices, the sin of envy. Where brotherly kindness flourishes, envy withers.

Of course, I'm not the first to speak on such things. A conversation about virtue's role in the Christian faith was under way long before I showed up. The medieval church, just as they categorized and codified sin into seven root vices, did the same with virtue. They called these, collectively, the Capital Virtues, and numbered them also at seven, each an antidote to one of the Seven Deadly Sins (or Capital Sins, as they were sometimes called).[4] For reasons beyond my historical or theological depth to explain, these seven virtues never attracted the same attention that the Seven Deadly Sins did. Virtue has never ignited humankind's curiosity, never captivated artists' and poets' imaginations, never awakened theological inquiry, quite like vice has. It's easier to remember the single Canto in Spenser's poem depicting the Sins than it is to recall the rest of the poem, which is about the acquisition of the Virtues. Such distraction and fixation in us might best be accounted for by the insidious nature of sin itself: Ever the impostor, brilliant at masquerade, sin bedazzles us in ways that virtue's outward drabness never does. We've always been more intrigued by fallen angels than six-winged seraphim.

But long before the medieval church did its theological groundwork on vice or virtue, there was Peter. Peter, writing to his little band of Christ-followers. Peter, a pastor concerned for men and women he knew by name, sheep and lambs whom Christ commanded him to feed. Peter, agonizing over his people's sufferings and wanderings, rejoicing when they stood fast.

Among them was (let's say) Detritus, a teenager rescued from the cult of Artemis but who kept wandering back to its central religious rite, sacred sex, or, for that matter, any sex he could dredge up. There was Bilious, a man whose chronic irritableness, repented of a thousand times, always seemed to get the upper hand at the worst moments—church board meetings, for example—and who left behind him a trail of hurt people, cut deep by his caustic tongue and barbed remarks. There was Odious, a woman who never did quite grasp the distinction between gossip and sharing, and so betrayed friend upon friend, blaming every one of them for the falling out.

And there was Peter, who'd traveled a long road to get here, wanting each of them and all of them to have *more*.

Is that what you want, *more*? If so, join me in discovering a treasure that for two thousand years has been hidden in plain sight, replete with old things to make life new.

2

Roots: Faith

THE BIBLE IS STRANGELY ASKEW. STRAIGHTFORWARD THINGS convolute, suddenly appearing to double back in contradiction. Proverbs, for instance: that's like a sock drawer of mismatched ideas—riches are good, or maybe bad; fools should be rebuked; no, fools should be avoided—and when you throw it side-by-side with Ecclesiastes, and mix in the Song of Songs, it's easy to get lost in the woods. Elsewhere, the Bible serves up a bland collection of tedious laws and plodding chronicles, then spices it up with a hot sauce of lurid tales, swashbuckling escapades, erotic trysts. The whole thing is by turns audacious then euphemistic, lucid then oblique, poetic then didactic.

It's hard to add it all up.

Try this:

You want to live? Die.

You desire to be great? Become little.

You aspire to rulership? Learn servility.

In the kingdom, firstness is lastness, poverty is riches, being cursed is being blessed. It takes a long time and a certain inner ear and many false starts to get used to this. It takes longer still to make any sense of it.

So depending on how long you've inhabited the Bible's strangely askew world, you will find Peter's opening remarks in his second letter either perfectly sensible, or borderline deranged.

His divine power has given us everything we need for life and godliness. . . . For this reason, make every effort . . . (2 Pet. 1:3a, 5a).

"We have everything we need" is how it begins. You have all that's required to live life to the hilt. "For this reason, make every effort" is how it continues. Strive to acquire what's needed to live life to the hilt.

Isn't this like saying, "You've got all the money you need. Therefore, try as hard as you can to get rich"?

Or is it? Maybe this is closer to common sense than first meets the eye. Something like this: *You have all the money you need for the life you want—only, invest it wisely and spend it with care. Don't squander it. Don't hoard it. Be generous. Be frugal. Be shrewd. Be honest.*

"You have all you need for life and godliness," Peter says. But it requires wise stewarding. It calls for diligence and discipline. Just because it's all there doesn't guarantee you'll put it to best use—or, for that matter, to any use at all. Some riches molder, never touched. Some are squandered, never treasured. Having all you need is not the same thing as making of it all you can.

The crucial word Peter uses here is *for*. God has given everything you need *for* life and godliness—*for* more. That tiny, solitary preposition implies huge responsibility. Imagine you were given everything you needed *for* a house. The land. The equipment to clear the land. The plans and permits, tools and materials. It's all there, down to the last galvanized screw and length of crown molding and strip of chimney flashing. The full inventory of supplies is at hand.

Everything you need *for* a house is intact.

All that's missing is you.

Now make every effort. Without that, wood weathers. Siding rots. Nails rust. Weeds flourish. Tools and machines oxidize. Years pass, and you're still living in the shed. Or, alternately, you might kick into action and take the tools and supplies and improvise something altogether of your own devising: a giant go-cart, a Trojan horse, a Tower of Babel.

Point's this: unless you make every effort toward the right thing, you can have everything you need and still end up with the wrong thing. God provides the entire inventory *for life and godliness*. That's the house to build. Anything less, anything else, is the wrong thing.

A HOUSE BEGINS WITH FOUNDATIONS. IF I'M TO MAKE EVERY effort to add virtue to my character—and every one of Peter's seven qualities are about character—what comes first? What's foundational, the groundwork I need to build upon?

Faith. "For this very reason, make every effort to *add to your faith.*" Faith is so basic that Peter doesn't pause at this juncture. He just assumes it's in place and barrels on past.

But I want to pause. The question of faith is crucial. Without faith it is impossible to please God. Whatever is done apart from faith—even good things—is sin. We walk but by faith, not sight. All this the Bible tells us. We can acquire virtue on virtue, a skyscraping tower of virtue, only to build it on sand or stilts, vulnerable to the next rough wind.

But we try it anyhow, virtue bereft of faith. It works for a spell.

But it always wears out, and wears us out. As a pastor, I get a weekly ringside seat on this: people striving to do the right thing, but feeling further and further from God. Like Martha, they're doing many good and needed things, but irritably, in a fever of mounting resentment and self-pity.

Virtue like that ends up no virtue at all.

Faith anchors virtue. Even more, faith releases it. It enlivens it, sustains it, directs it. It ignites it with altar fire. Put bluntly, it is impossible to be good without God. We might get the effort off the ground, but like a stub-winged bird born only to waddle, we can't stay airborne long. Faithless virtue is short-lived and, ultimately, futile.

So what is faith?

Here's how Peter begins his second letter:

> Simon Peter, a servant and apostle of Jesus Christ, To those who through the righteousness of our God and Savior Jesus Christ have received a faith as precious as ours. (2 Pet. 1:1)

"To those who . . . have received a faith as precious as ours."

Two things leap out: faith is a gift, and faith is a treasure. As a gift, we can only receive it. As treasure, we ought to, well, treasure it.

Faith is a gift that comes to us mysteriously, undeserved, unexpected. It cannot be bought, borrowed, or conjured, but you can ask for it. That seems a double bind—to ask a God we don't believe in for faith to believe. But it's a double bind that works, a knot tied twice that somehow unravels itself.

My own story's instructive. I grew up with a father angry at the church for no particular reason and a mother who, for most of my childhood, chased swamis. I had a beggar's notion of God, scavenged from rumors and guesses. My faith, such as it was, was laden with superstition and riddled with doubt. I prayed, as children do, out of some vestigial instinct, prayers that were mostly panic or greed cloaked in flattery and bargain making, like I was trying to persuade a tyrant given to caprices of freak generosity to give me half his kingdom. When I was about sixteen, my mother came to faith, and soon after my brother did as well. That puzzled and disturbed me and also, though I fought it hard, intrigued me. It began to work in me a gravitational pull.

I started to long for faith to believe. But I had so many questions, the usual kinds, but questions that no one I asked could answer, at least to my satisfaction—questions about the nature of God (Is he three or one? Is he good but weak? Powerful but indifferent?), questions about his ways (Why shouldn't good people, on the basis of their goodness, get to go to heaven? Why do the innocent suffer?). Everyone to whom I pitched such questions tossed back answers that struck me as glib or clumsy, loosely memorized from some dumbed-down apologetics manual. So I was frustrated and found Christians an easy alibi for why I wasn't one.

But still, I found myself pulled toward God. Something was taking shape inside of me that my unbelief could no longer absorb. One or the other had to go. And then one day it came to a crisis: Could I believe in a God I didn't yet believe in? I didn't know, I wasn't sure. But I asked anyhow, asked for faith, asked the God I lacked confidence in to impart to me the confidence to have confidence in him (if that makes sense, and even today, more than twenty-five years later, it only partly does to me).

But that's exactly what God did: he took this quarter-formed and half-baked thing inside me—a mix of wonderment and wistfulness and dread—and turned it into faith, faith in the Son of God.

It was sheer gift.

BUT NOW I TREASURE IT. IT IS UNSPEAKABLY PRECIOUS. THE Greek word for "precious" is *isotimos*, its root *timios*. It's a word typically used to describe jewels—rubies, emeralds, diamonds. Keepsakes and heirlooms, things rare and costly. Things desired, and once gained, cherished.

Faith as precious as ours. Peter describes it that way, not to mean that some people get a more valuable portion of faith than others—some get jewels, others gravel. He means that some people know the true value of the gift. They know how precious it is.

One way to learn how to treasure faith is to get close to people who already do. Find someone whose faith in Christ is everything to them, someone who lives and breathes it, someone who would take a bullet through the head before they would turn away from the God who loves them. Faith erodes when we walk in the counsel of the wicked, or stand in the way of sinners, or sit in the seat of mockers. It deteriorates in the company of the indolent. But it shines when run in the path of the upright.

At one of our church's men's retreats, the speaker, Steve Wilson, told about visiting the Ukraine in the early '90s and meeting a man whose right hand was a stump of twisted flesh. Steve kept staring at it, and the man's grown son noticed. "You are wondering what happened to my father's hand?"

"Yes."

"Before the fall of communism, he was imprisoned for his faith.

Every week, the guards came and told him he must renounce his faith or they would cut off a finger. The first week, they cut off his baby finger. The next, his thumb. The next, his ring finger. They eventually cut off his whole hand before they realized that this was getting them nowhere. He would lose anything, everything, before he would deny Jesus."

A faith as precious as ours.

THE BOOK OF HEBREWS, THAT GLORIOUS ANTHEM, HELPS US grasp the substance of faith by giving us three touchstones for it.

Famously, to begin, is the opening of Hebrews 11.

> Now faith is being sure of what we hope for and certain of what we do not see. This is what the ancients were commended for.
>
> By faith we understand that the universe was formed at God's command, so that what is seen was not made out of what was visible. (Heb. 11:1-3)

The bedrock of faith is the conviction that what matters most is more than matter. The material world, the stuff I touch and see and smell, is not the "real world." The real word is unseen. Things visible are actually made from and sustained by things unseen. A rock, a flower, a bird, a child—all blossom out of and are rooted in a world beyond the world. God spoke, things appeared. A geologist might tell you that a rock came from an amalgam of minerals accumulating over eons, fused together in earth's hot, dark kiln, pried back into daylight by water's patience and violence. An ornithologist might account for a bird by an intricate story of blind force and blind luck, the happy if unlikely outcome of cruelty and serendipity. But neither can tell you what happened first. Both must stand mute before the wonder of ultimate beginnings.

But Hebrews and Genesis are not mute. They tell us that before anything existed there was a voice crying in the wilderness. Words danced in emptiness and brimmed with life, and from sheer nothingness sprang rock and water, fruit and feather, hide and hoof.

And the voice still speaks, and all things, and you besides, live and move and have their being because of it.

What matters is more than matter.

This conviction is not oriented just to the past, but also poised toward the future. Hebrews 11:10, describing the faith of Abraham, says he was "looking *forward* to the city with foundations, whose architect and builder is God." Faith is the substance of things *hoped* for. The faithful walk, not by sight, but by the conviction that what we see is not what we get, not then and not now and not ever. They believe that the creation emerged out of things unseen, but also that it moves toward things beyond imagining.

The musician Ray Charles went blind at age seven. Something gathered over his eyes, turned his world grainy and gray, finally closed him in utter darkness. He lived his childhood in rural poverty, in a one-room shack at the edge of a sharecropper's field. In the movie about him, in a scene from his childhood, he runs into his house and trips over a chair. He starts to wail for his mother. She stands at the stove, right in front of him, and instinctively reaches out to lift him. Then she stops. Backs up. Stands still. Watches.

Ray stops crying. He quiets. He listens. He hears, behind him, the water on the wood stove whistling to a boil. He hears, outside, the wind pass like a hand through cornstalks. He hears the thud of horse hooves on the road, the creak and clatter of the wagon they pull.

Then he hears, in front of him, the thin faint scratch of a grasshopper walking the worn floorboards of his mama's cottage. He inches over and, attentive now to every sigh and twitch, gathers the tiny insect in his hand. He holds it in his open palm. "I hear you, too, Mama," he says. She weeps with pride and sorrow and wonder.

Later he explains to someone, "I hear like you see."[1]

That's faith's motto: *I hear like you see.* I trust in God—in what he's done and is doing and will do—as much, even more, as others trust in what they touch and taste and see.

What we see is not what we get.

But there's more.

> And without faith it is impossible to please God, because anyone who comes to him must believe that he exists and that he rewards those who earnestly seek him. (Heb. 11:6)

That single verse brings together two other aspects of biblical faith: the faithful believe God exists, and he rewards those who pursue him. They believe, quite simply, that God *is* and that he's good.

The first part appears so simplistic as to almost require no commentary. Of course faith believes God is. What else would it be?

But it's not as obvious as it first appears. Some things mimic faith but are really diluted or counterfeit forms of it. Faith *in* faith, for instance, where the object of faith is faith itself, or something so vague as to render our feelings toward it no more than sentiment or superstition. I often get into spiritual conversations with people on airplanes. I've met very few people who outright reject faith *in something*—the broad term for this now is *spirituality*—and many of them profess to a "deep faith." I'm not out to pick a fight, but I sometimes ask what they mean.

"What do you have faith *in*?" I ask.

The question stumps most people.

"What do you mean?"

"Well," I say, "what if I told you that I have faith in this airplane?"

"Well, I do too. I wouldn't have boarded it otherwise."

"Right. But at that point, you've filled in a few blanks: what you think I mean is that I have faith in the soundness of the plane's design, its construction, its material, its maintenance, its fuel supply. I have faith in the people operating it. I have faith in the people on the ground giving instructions to get it up and get it down in one piece. Is that right?"

"Sure."

"But what if I told you my faith was otherwise—that my faith in this plane means I believe it could fly without its engines running. Or that it could fly on its own. Or that it could land on top of a high-rise. What would you think then?"

"You're nuts."

"You wouldn't fly with me if I was the pilot and had that kind of faith?"

"No."

"Fair enough. But to claim faith yet remain vague about what that faith is in—isn't that sort of the same thing?"

Of course, I try to do this in playfulness and friendliness. I'm not looking to embarrass anyone, myself or anyone else. I just want to do a little Socratic sparring, to bring to the surface assumptions buried, unexamined, maybe fallacy-riddled. The truth is, faith's value is rooted in the soundness and worthiness of its object. Without faith, it's impossible to please God; but without God, it's impossible to have good faith. Faith has nowhere to lay its head.

But a more common problem, at least within churches, is faith without deeds: otherwise orthodox belief that rarely asks the question, *How then shall we live?* Its hidden motto is, *Believe, but carry on as usual*. We often divide people on the God question between *theists* and *atheists*—between those who believe in God and those who don't. We need a third category: *apatheists*. That's *apathy* joined to *theism*, indifference married to creed.[2] Apatheists believe in God but don't really care. They're glad God is out there, somewhere, doing something, hearing prayers and spinning planets. But his existence impinges little on their own. It doesn't guide their actions, shape their decisions, correct their attitudes. God is no present, urgent reality: he's a distant, occasionally interesting idea. (We'll look more closely at this problem in the next chapter.)

True faith believes God is. He exists. His existence is the one reality that explains, defines, and is able to redeem every other reality. His is the one existence upon which all other existences depend. In him we live, and move, and have our being.

But true faith also believes God *rewards those who earnestly seek him*. It's the conviction that nothing is more gratifying than pursuing the invisible God. Jesus warned us not to chase after the things of this world: stuff and pleasure and money and status. Put bluntly, we're not to go after the "good life," at least our usual version of that. Are we then to pursue the "bad life"—hardship, loneliness, poverty? Well, in a manner of speaking, yes. Blessed are the poor, Jesus said, the hungry, the blamed, the mocked.

But Jesus said that as a sweeping indictment of a life that promises the world, or a sizable chunk of it, but parches the souls. Jesus exposed the fraudulence of what we call *the good life*. We chase things that don't last. We accumulate treasures that the destroying trinity of moth and thief and rust devour. We might gain everything we want and lose the one thing we need. Jesus abruptly interrupts that vain pursuit and shows a better way: seek first God's kingdom and righteousness.

But that requires believing God is good. God *is* the good life. He is not out to ruin us. God does not try, by tricks and threats, to sleuth out the thing you dread most, then foist it on you or press-gang you into it. *Oh, you don't want to be a missionary in outer Mongolia? Wait until you see the surprise I've got waiting for you . . .* It is true that a life of seeking God is harder, harder by far, than a life of going your own way. But that's only for a season, and then the terms reverse, radically and utterly and extravagantly. I have been walking with Jesus for more than twenty-five years. I would not exchange my worst day with Jesus for my best day without him.

And the best is yet to come.

Three things, then, are the substance of faith: the conviction that what matters most are things unseen; the conviction that God exists—he is the one reality that every other reality bows to and lives by; and the conviction that the pursuit of God *is* the good life, a life not only richly rewarding, but whose rewards are the only ones you can keep forever—indeed, the only ones you would want to keep forever.

TWO SUMMERS AGO, MY FAMILY AND I VISITED THE CANADIAN side of Niagara Falls. I was unprepared for my own astonishment—my sense of utter smallness in the presence of water and rock. I was agog at the wild terror and pure beauty of it, the spectacle of white torrent hurtling into deep chasm. I decreased, and God and his creation increased. We stood a long time, my wife and three children and I, in the drenching mist that rises up, day and night, from water crashing against water. We took the boat ride that swept us, sheathed in plastic, a stone's shot from the fall's crushing veil.

But we never traveled south of the border, to the American side. I understand that a mile upstream from where we stood, the Welland River joins the Niagara River. Right where those two rivers meet, a passenger bridge arches across the Welland. Boaters can navigate beneath this bridge and enter the wide flow of the Niagara. But just before they do, they pass under a large sign posted on the bridge's pylon. It asks them two questions:

Do you have an anchor?

Do you know how to use it?[3]

Every virtue we will look at in this book—seven old things to make life new—will be as vulnerable as a rowboat in white water if not anchored in faith. Without that, all we gain can be quickly swept away.

Do you have faith?

Do you know how to use it?

The Petrine Diaries:
Increase Our Faith

THE APOSTLE PETER UNNERVES BECAUSE HE RESEMBLES ME, like a brother from a different mother, like a spiritual dead ringer. We can both be by turns rash, dithering, cocky, cowering. We have a knack for leaping off the start line and hobbling to the finish. We often say things we don't mean and mean things we don't say. The good we want to do we leave undone, and the evil we don't want to do we pratfall right into. We act swiftly, impetuously, many times disastrously, against our better instincts. And then we fail to act at precisely those moments both wisdom and courage demand it. We think that saying something noble or valiant is the same thing as doing something noble and valiant. We cherish the appearance of virtue, even if we lack the virtue itself. We can be, the two of us, eloquent and emphatic in our own defense, mumble-mouthed in Jesus's defense.

But Jesus liked him anyhow, and hard knock by hard knock put spiritual backbone and sinew into him. I think it's just so with me.

Peter had a habit of overstepping himself. He longed to display holiness and faithfulness, but more times than not tripped into a burlesque of backpedaling and second-guessing. He built a tower of heroic self-image on the stilts of rickety character. And so his intent, all grandeur and valor, often collapsed under its own weight. He bandied words like *never* and *always* but got stuck in a pattern of *maybe* and *sometimes*. He said things such as, *No matter what*, that really meant, *If it suits me at the time.*

And yet, despite all that, he desperately wanted to get it right. The first lesson he had to learn, and the last, and the lesson all the way in between, was that of faith: that without faith it is impossible to please God. That faith comes from *hearing*—it's neither derived from nor exercised by *seeing*. That we walk by faith, not by sight.

We either advance by the voice of Christ beckoning, or sink at the sight of waves rising. We either stand our ground by Christ's voice speaking in our inmost places, or abandon our post at the mere accusation of a servant girl.

In Matthew's Gospel, Peter asks Jesus a straightforward question. "How many times should I forgive my brother when he sins against me?" (Matt. 18: 21). This is a good question. It's practical and realistic, not rhetorical or moot in any way. Peter puts his finger on a point where the Christian life often falters—the trickiness and prickliness of human relationship. He names a real problem, hard to unravel and all too familiar: the presence of the repeat offender.

Every community has them. They breed trouble in stealthy ways and turn communities—homes, offices, shops, churches—into hotbeds of backbiting and rumor-mongering. Wherever two or three gather, there they are also, stirring up divisiveness in the very places Jesus seeks to bring oneness. If they themselves are aware of how much damage they do, they don't let on: they're masterful at feigning ignorance, pleading innocence.

How long do you put up with them? How many times do you forgive them, despite all their hangdog gestures and heartfelt apologies or outright denials, when they keep doing damage? Peter suggests a number: up to seven times (Matt. 18:21–22).

Which seems to me extravagant.

But Jesus finds it paltry. He thinks it's stingy. He's got a number in mind, one of staggering proportions: depending on how you read it, seventy-seven times, or seventy times seven, meaning 490 times—either way, a number too large to count on two hands and all your toes.

Behind Jesus's words is an allusion to Lamech, thrice-great grandson of Cain and high priest of the cult of vengeance. *I have killed a man for wounding me, a young man for injuring me*, he boasts, creed-like. *If Cain is avenged seven times, I am avenged seventy-seven times* (Gen. 4:23–24; emphasis mine). This is bitter irony. Cain killed his own brother with no higher motive than jealousy. It was cold and premeditated. Yet in Lamech's eyes, Cain was justified—merely avenging himself. Thus, Lamech reasons, his own actions are virtually obligatory. For him, vendetta on a grand scale, retaliation for even the slightest provocation, is the best and maybe the only way to deal with one who sins against us. Jesus invokes Lamech's number but subverts his creed. He annuls the law of retaliation and replaces it, scandalously, with the law of forgiveness.

Jesus also indulges here in typical rabbinical hyperbole. The number, its sheer extravagance, is meant to startle, just like Jesus's talk about removing logs from eyes and blind guides straining out gnats and camels slipping through the eyes of needles. Jesus is more intent on shocking Peter into a new way of seeing than he is on giving him a working number. He wants to shatter all Peter's ledger-keeping strictures, all his fair-minded, commonsensical ways of dealing with others. He wants to incite a revolution in his heart.

But he's aghast, Peter is, and with him the other disciples. That's how I read the variation on this story in Luke's Gospel. In that account, no one asks Jesus a question—Jesus simply segues from a discussion about the seriousness of sin to the seriousness of forgiveness. Sin, he says, should be treated with harsh and unflinching consequences: *It would be better for [anyone] to be thrown into the sea with a millstone tied around his neck than . . . to cause one of these little ones to sin. So watch yourselves* (Matt. 18:6). Just as his disciples might be doing tabulations on that, Jesus interrupts with this:

> If your brother sins, rebuke him, and if he repents, forgive him. If
> he sins against you seven times in a day, and seven times comes back
> to you and says, "I repent," forgive him. (Luke 17:3–4)

This is exhausting and seemingly fruitless, this cycle of sin, rebuke, repentance, forgiveness, seven times a day, seven days a week. At some point, we ought to call the offender's bluff. We ought to keep from falling for this tired song and dance. We ought to stop "enabling" the offender, being "codependent" with him or her, making excuses. Insanity, therapists tell us, is doing the same thing over and over and expecting different results. Grace, we'd think, must wear a different visage under these circumstances.

But Peter and the others don't stand and argue with Jesus (give them their due—I can't imagine myself swallowing this without a fight). They simply accept Jesus's math, but ask him for one thing besides: "Increase our faith!" (Luke 17:5).

Were I there, I might have asked for something else: "Give us better sociopsychological models to grasp the inner dynamics of this man's behavior. Increase our capacity to create broad yet precise policies for dealing with human dysfunction. Impart a more integrated and holistic paradigm of spiritual formation. Provide us with more potent and symptom-specific medications. Enlarge our tolerance."

Come to think of it, no. I like Peter and company's response: *Increase our faith*. Help us, each and all, to see and believe more deeply what God is up to in the thickness and thinness of our fallen lives, the awkwardness and messiness of broken people living together. Help us find the Spirit in the midst of our tiredness and testiness, our heartbreak and disappointment. Come fresh to us and renew us in God's grace when all our natural goodwill gets buried beneath our hurt and anger.

What life calls for is not, first and foremost, more cunning, more skill, more resources. It calls for more faith.

That day, Peter—astonished at the largeness of Jesus's number, at the wideness of God's mercy—grasped a simple, shocking truth: without faith, it's not only impossible to please God. Without it, in the end it's impossible even to have a friend.

3

Root and Branch: Faith and Works

IN 1959, THE USSR LEADER NIKITA KHRUSHCHEV MADE AN unprecedented visit to America. This was right after the death of Russian dictator Joseph Stalin, and Khrushchev, his successor, had already caused a global stir by denouncing in Russia, in a long and intricately detailed speech to the Politburo, Stalin's many atrocities: his genocidal policies against the Ukraine, his cold-blooded assassinations of toadies, informers, wonks, lieutenants—anyone who had become "redundant," whose existence no longer served "the party"—his purges, both random and systematic, of anyone he didn't trust, which was almost everyone.

Khrushchev was scheduled to appear at the National Press Club in Washington. It was widely expected he would deliver an abbreviated version of his Politburo speech. Every newspaper and magazine of any standing made sure they had at least one reporter present. The room was packed. Khrushchev did not disappoint: he delivered, via translator, a shortened but potent indictment of his former boss, complete with corroborating evidence.

He finished and opened the floor for questions. Someone called out from the crowd, "Mr. Khrushchev, you have just given us an account of Mr. Stalin's many crimes against humanity. You were his right-hand man during much of that. What were you doing?"

The question was translated to Khrushchev, and when he heard it he exploded with anger. "Who said that?" he demanded.

No one answered.

"Who said that?" he bellowed, and glowered at the audience.

Silence.

"Who said that?" he asked again, this time low and quiet, with more menace.

Everyone looked at their shoes.

After a moment, Khrushchev said, *"That's* what I was doing."[1]

Jesus says that on the Day of Judgment, he will tell his true followers by a single touchstone: they translated faith into action. When the suffering of the least of these came to their attention, they did not turn away. They did not just look at their shoes. No matter what it cost or where it led, they said, "Here I am. Send me."

Their faith produced works.

It's what true faith does.

JOSEPH FIENNES MAKES A SMOOTH-SKINNED MARTIN LUTHER. In a recent movie about Luther, Fiennes plays the famous monk-turned-Reformer with delicacy of manner and refinement of feeling. It's like Esau pretending to be Jacob. He has a wounded frailty about him, a child's fragile wistfulness. Even his torments seem but love throes, his anger only the froth of heartbreak.

He's very thin.

We miss the real Luther, the man burly and coarse, with dyspeptic temper, Rabelaisian humor, oafish manners: the brusque and belching former monk, part bonhomie and part curmudgeon, slurring out slurs against Jews and popes, knocking back his pint of thick, dark ale and ripping his barley loaf with stained teeth, happy as Bacchus to have thrown off the austerities of the monastery to embrace the messy pleasures of domestic life. We miss the man's sheer brawling vitality and his deep, brooding intensity. We miss his holy dishevelment and utter abundance, the endearing rough-hewness of the man.

Luther is famous for his dictum *Sola fide*—"by faith alone." By faith alone we come to Christ. We stagger bankrupt to the cross, with nothing in our hands worth keeping, only discarding. We come not to be commended, only forgiven.

But what forgiveness we find there. It sears and cleanses, plumbs the depths, scours the dregs, and scrubs to brilliant white every last little stain. Christ's forgiveness speaks truth in the inmost parts, and there is no word that need or can be added after it has spoken. It is finished.

All this by faith alone.

Luther was ever vigilant about that. Any hint that there was some other work or word required to secure God's favor was anathema to him. He would stand down councils, defy popes, suffer exile, risk death rather than give ground on that.

So after a time, a caricature of Luther took shape. He was depicted as the gadfly of goodness and the foe of good works. He was pilloried as a carnival barker for lawlessness and debauchery. He was seen as the enemy of virtue.

This image persisted, even among Luther's own ilk, deep into the last century. I remember as a teen, back in the early '70s, watching a television debate between two Lutheran ministers. (It's funny that I should have watched this, and that it should have stuck in my memory, given my distinctly irreligious early years.)

The debate, moderated by a gaunt man in a pencil-thin suit, pitted an older minister, frocked and dignified, against a young one, smocked and flippant. The young minister took to taunting the older man, and the older man rebuffed him with schoolmarm sternness. It was like a street punk taking on an aging aristocrat, a brawler spoiling for a fight, just for fun, pairing off against a man accustomed to pistol duels, for the sake of defending honor among gentlemen.

What I remember most was the older man taking the young man to task for his loose morals, and the young man's retort:

"Sin boldly. Sin boldly. Do you know who said that?"

"No."

"Luther said that. Our great leader, Martin Luther. He said that."

"I don't believe it."

"Well he did. You could look it up. Sin boldly."

The young minister leaned back, smug, triumphant. The old minister looked discomfited, tired and bewildered, ready to go home.

I did look it up, a long time after. The young minister was right; Luther did say that: *Sin boldly*—or, in a likely more accurate rendering, *Let your sin be strong*. But what the young minister neglected to say, or maybe didn't know or care enough to say, was what else Luther had to say in and around his otherwise stark and puzzling imperative. The context of Luther's statement was how life itself implicates us in sin and compromise: just getting out of bed this morning was an act of thrusting a fallen man into a sin-wracked world, and some no-good thing was bound to come from it. My embrace of one task requires my neglect of another. A word in season to one person may come as a word of disruption to another, just as every *yes* entails a *no*. The money I spend on bread or milk may, hither-tither, line the pocket of someone somewhere who will use it to buy guns for killing street kids in Brazil.

There is no waking up without some falling out. Every good deed sets in motion a chain of reactions, some of which will, by hook or by crook, make havoc. Every trip to the temple will be at the expense of some poor blighter not lifted out of a ditch, and every person lifted out of a ditch has unforeseen consequences: blood on the upholstery, a debt on the Visa card, a spouse angry that you're late again for dinner, a potential codependency. Here are some real-life examples. Christian programs to buy the freedom of women and children sold into slavery in Asia and Africa have created a growth market in abductions: people who never thought of slave trading now nab the vulnerable so they can sell them back to Christians. Or shoeboxes stuffed with toothbrushes and pencils, sent to impoverished children in some hard-pressed country, undermine that country's local economy: some honest businessman trying to sell toothbrushes and pencils in that village has just lost a year's worth of revenue. Or a church's prayerful decision to release funds for the much-needed repair of the chancery means that the much-depleted food bank goes begging. On and on it goes.

You can't wake up without some fallout. *Sin boldly*, Luther said in response. Don't let life's inherent complexity, its pact with the devil, keep you from doing anything. If every act, intended for the best of ends, is sinful anyhow, then sin boldly. Don't anguish over every last little thing. Do what needs doing, and leave the outcome to God.

Here's what Luther actually wrote:

If you are a preacher of mercy, do not preach an imaginary but the true mercy. If the mercy is true, you must therefore bear the true, not an imaginary sin. God does not save those who are only imaginary sinners. Be a sinner, and let your sins be strong [sin boldly], but let your trust in Christ be stronger, and rejoice in Christ who is the victor over sin, death, and the world. We will commit sins while we are here, for this life is not a place where justice resides. We, however, says Peter [2 Pet. 3:13] are looking forward to a new heaven and a new earth where justice will reign.[2]

As one translation of this puts it: "Sin boldly, but trust in Christ more boldly still." This is Christian realism at its best married to theological confidence at its highest. If Christ accepts us by something other than faith alone, we're doomed from the outset. There simply cannot be, not for you, me, or anyone, enough stacking up of good deeds to equal eternal reward. If God's forgiveness hinges on a pair of scales, where virtue must outweigh vice, quit now, while you're only this far behind. But thank God it doesn't hinge on that. It is staked, top to bottom, on a cross, where only one man died. A cross where sins aren't measured; they're canceled. Where good deeds aren't applauded; they're canceled too. Thank God our salvation depends, only and utterly, on Christ's mercy toward you and me, sinners both.

By faith alone.

YET LUTHER DIDN'T DISMISS THE IMPORTANCE OF GOOD WORKS. He wanted, forever and a day, to put them and keep them in their rightful place. He refused to bestow on them an honor God himself denies them. But he was not the enemy of virtue that his enemies, and some of his so-called friends, made him out to be. Here, for example, is a typical sampling of his reflections on the relationship between faith and works. Citing John 15:17, "This is my command: Love each other," Luther wrote:

> By love, believers are held together, and love is the mark of true believers. Jesus emphasized this command because he knew how many false Christians would arise—how many would praise faith with elegant words and make a great show but wouldn't back up their words. . . . Christ teaches us that it's not enough to praise faith and Christ, but we also need to produce Christian fruit. For where the fruits aren't evident, or where their opposite appears, Christ is certainly not present. . . . But some will object, "Doesn't faith justify and save us without works?" Yes, that's true. But where's your faith? How does it show itself? Faith must never be useless, deaf, dead, or in a state of decay. But it must be a living tree that bursts forth with fruit. That's the difference between genuine faith and false faith. Where there is true faith, it will show itself in a person's life.[3]

Or this, on another occasion:

> We should always remember that where there is no faith, there can be no good works, and where there are no good works, there is no faith. Therefore, we must keep faith and good works connected. The entire Christian life is embodied by both.[4]

Faith is both in the roots and the branches. As Jesus himself said, you can tell a true prophet—the man or woman who genuinely knows God and speaks for God—by his or her fruit (Matt. 7). Thorn bushes don't grow grapes. Thistles don't sprout figs. Good trees produce good fruit, and bad trees bad, or none at all.

What is in the roots shows up among the leaves.

THIS ROOT-AND-BRANCH NATURE OF TRUE FAITH IS EMBEDDED in Peter's call to virtue. He assumes, as we've seen, that without faith it's impossible to please God. Faith is the root system. Without it, there is form only, devoid of life.

Yet *it must be a living tree that bursts forth with fruit.* Life depends on the roots, and yet a tree, no matter how well rooted, that never matures into fruitfulness is good only for mulch or firewood.

This is the whole point Peter is making when he enjoins us to "make every effort *to add* to your faith . . ." Add what? Fruit. As James put it, faith without works is dead. As Luther had it, faith without fruit is false.

Of course, to carry on the tree-and-fruit metaphor, apple trees don't strive to grow apples. It's just what they do. I have an apple tree, and a plum too, and a cherry, and not once have I seen any of them making anything that resembles an effort to bear fruit. Every year, there they are, a foot or two taller, another ring thicker. Each new spring finds them bristling with a denser cluster of buds, each summer crowned with a wilder tumult of leaves, each fall drooping with a weightier crop of fruit. Not once have I seen any of them strive to do it.

Yet the conditions must be right. Soil, climate, location, irrigation, fertilization, pruning, cross-pollination: all play significant roles. And maybe that's what Peter means when he tells us to make every effort—he's simply telling us, in Annie Dillard's words, "to be mindful of conditions." He's reminding us that we shape, if not the environment in which fruit is grown, at least the conditions under which it can flourish.

Faith has fruit to bear. Faith alone can get us to heaven, but its purpose between now and then is to birth something in us that makes a difference on earth. There are hungry people to feed, some closer than you think. There are single mothers, bone-tired and dirt-poor, to encourage. Some go to your church. There are people in hospitals, and prisons, and care homes. They need visits. Some of them you're related to. There are neighbors—that's the person across the fence from you—who could use a kind word, or help in the yard, or just a friend to drink a cup of tea with.

As Peter found, the deeds faith calls us to do are usually as ordinary and unglamorous as feeding sheep.

I sometimes relish the idea of giving away a million dollars in one grand flourish to some great cause. What I resist is giving away a million dollars, or even a thousand, in dribs and drabs to the least of these. The first is the stuff of heart-thumping heroism, the second bone-scraping sacrifice. The first is a kind of glorious martyrdom, the second a kind of obscure and slow death. But Jesus told us to die a little every day—every day, take up your cross and follow him. Every day do as Paul did: *carry around the death of Jesus, so that the life of Jesus might be available to others* (2 Cor. 4:10–11).

This is the fruit of faith, these small but significant acts of Christlikeness. Be mindful of the conditions that grow such fruit. The best way I've figured to do that is to cultivate the attitudes of my heart. Christlike works that heal a broken world are borne in Christlike humility. Why Mother Teresa probably did more earthly good than the entire UN has something to do with this. Why bureaucracy and machinery and medicine may treat illness, but only another human acting in genuine concern can deeply heal it, has something to with this. Why psychology can name and explain a torment, but only love can cast it out, has something to do with this.

The conditions under which fruitfulness increases are matters of the heart. And such attitudes are cultivated by one thing only: closeness to Jesus. "If a man remains in me and I in him, he will bear much fruit; apart from me you can do nothing" (John 15:5). There is no way to do Christlike acts except by way of intimacy with Christ himself. I must live in Jesus, and let his Word live in me. I must listen to him, be heedful of him. If ever I'm to do Martha-like acts with real effect, I must do it with Mary-like submissiveness and attentiveness to Jesus.

PAT CONROY'S NOVEL *THE PRINCE OF TIDES* TELLS THE TANGLED story, generations long, of the gifted but deeply flawed Wingo family. In one chapter, Tom Wingo recounts the WWII ordeal his father, Henry, endured after his plane plummeted, tail wings aflame, over German soil. Injured and fugitive, Henry takes refuge in a Catholic church. The church's priest, Father Günter Kraus, is a good man but timid, and when he discovers Henry in his vestry, bloody and delirious, he's torn between his compassion and his fear. He wants to help, but he's terrified of the consequences should the Nazis find out he's harboring an enemy. Tom Wingo says,

> My father's presence had created a moral nightmare for the priest and it tested the mettle of his character. The priest felt he had been given the soul of a rabbit in times that called for lions. . . . My father's coming had required the priest in him to rule over the man."[5]

My father's coming had required the priest in him to rule over the man. Which is what the Father's coming requires also in us. Christ has made us "a kingdom and priests to serve his God and Father"

(Rev. 1:6). He has made us a "royal priesthood" (1 Pet. 2:9). He himself is the great high priest, and he lives, to rule and reign, in all those who call on his name (Heb. 4:14–5:10).

In an age that calls for lions, let the priest in you rule over the man.

The Petrine Diaries:
Let Us Put Up Three Shelters

PETER HAD A MOUNTAINTOP EXPERIENCE TO TRUMP ALL OTHERS, and nearly ruined it by a silly outburst. He watched Jesus change before his eyes, from earthly peasant to heavenly icon, radiant with otherworldly beauty. He watched two ancient spiritual giants, Moses and Elijah, descend from mystic heights and stand with Jesus, confer with him, defer to him. There were James and John alongside, witnessing a theophany to rival Ezekiel's by the river Kebar, to surpass Isaiah's in Jerusalem's temple. But unlike those men, whom the vision stunned into silence or woe, Peter started chattering.

> Peter said to Jesus, "Rabbi, it is good for us to be here. Let us put up three shelters—one for you, one for Moses and one for Elijah." (He did not know what to say, they were so frightened). (Mark 9:5–6)

Mark adds the parenthetical comment by way of excuse.

The man who once seemed to resent Jesus for meddling in the fishing trade (see Luke 5:1–5) suddenly fancied himself a carpenter after the Master's own heart. The man who would later have an ambivalent relationship with the apostle Paul now wanted to try his own hand at tent making.

Peter's comment has a comical edge to it, like a one-liner from a

Laurel and Hardy routine or an antic out of an *I Love Lucy* episode. It's a Mr. Bean gag, an uproarious bit of slapstick—a pauper's audience with royalty going outlandishly awry, a man-on-the-street's meeting with the president being marred by some shocking gaffe.

Hilarious.

Only, I'm rethinking all that. Peter at least got this much right: he knew that revelation entails response. A manifestation of the divine demands some version of "Here I am. Send me" (see Isa. 6). Peter may have blundered and stammered. He may have been scared spitless and harebrained, but at least he lurched toward worship and service. Like an old mouser gone arthritic, his instincts were intact even if his reflexes were clumsy. He knew that if Jesus entrusted to him a glimpse of the glory to be revealed, then something was bound to be asked of him.

Rashly, he offers to build something *for this moment.*

Wisely, he knows to build something *out of this moment.*

Fear produces his response. But faith is entwined with it: If God has done this for me, shown this much to me, what can I do for him? *To whom much has been given,* Jesus said, *much is required* (Luke 12:48). Like Paul, who was given "surpassingly great revelations" (2 Cor. 12:7) and who as a consequence declared, "I will very gladly spend for you everything I have and expend myself as well" (v. 15) Peter's surpassingly great revelation led to a glad willingness to spend and expend himself. Out of the abundance of what he'd received, he knew to build something.

"His divine power has given us everything we need for life and godliness," Peter wrote much later. "For this very reason, *make every effort . . .*"

I think this lesson became clearest for Peter late in his discipleship to Jesus—just prior to Christ's crucifixion and just after his resurrection. Two episodes come to mind, both only recorded by John in his Gospel. The first is the Last Supper, where Jesus, knowing God has put all authority under him, stoops and washes his disciples' feet. Peter at first wants no part of this. But Jesus explains that unless he washes Peter's feet, Peter can have no part of him. So then Peter wants a dousing, a head-to-toe shower. *No,* Jesus tells him, *I've already done that for you, cleaned you up top-to-bottom, inside out. It's just that your feet keep accumulating muck and grime. It's hard to walk through this world without getting a little of the world on you. So you're going to need a footbath on a regular basis.*

Then Jesus sits back and instructs his disciples about what's just happened. "I have set you an example," he says, "that you should do as I have done for you. . . . Now that you know these things, you will be blessed if you do them" (John 13:15, 17).

There are a few ways, I suppose, we might make meaning out of this. One is to "build a booth" around this moment: to institutionalize foot washing, make it sacramental. I'm not disdaining such practice, but it does seem to me to miss something more essential going on here. Nowhere do we have any hint that the early church enshrined foot washing this way. That came later.

The more essential meaning is that we serve others by helping them clean the world off themselves: the little bits of gossip we pick up in the workplace, the overstimulation we absorb in a sex-saturated culture, the self-centeredness we imbibe in the push-and-shove of everyday living. I need this scrubbed off me every few days, and I usually need someone's help to get to the undersides of things, the hard-to-reach places, the tight little crooks and joints where grime hides, and builds, and rots.

This is dirty work, washing feet. It's menial. It feels beneath us.

But it's what the faithful do for one another. It's the kind of good work faith produces.

The other episode I have in mind is on the lakeshore, after the Resurrection. Jesus asks Peter three times, *Do you love me?* When Peter says he does, Jesus simply commands him, *"Feed my sheep"* (John 21:17–19).

Love and faith express themselves in good works. Love, faith— they look for something to do: wash feet, feed sheep.

Build shelters.

There are moments when Christ, crouching in humility or glowing in splendor, meets us. Out of such moments, we build something—not to preserve the moment, but to live out its meaning for those who weren't there.

You should do as I have done for you. You will be blessed if you do.

4

Not by Might: Faith and Spirit

I ALWAYS IMAGINED SAMSON OX-LIKE IN GIRTH. TALL AS
Goliath, brawny as Hercules. He is, in my mind, a hulking, scowl-
ing brute of a man, iron-hewn with muscle: muscle coiling out his
ears, braiding down his limbs, crosshatched across his chest. Muscle
mounded dense and hard on every last inch of him. Fists big like
mallets, crowned with knuckles large as lug nuts. If he strode into
the room, you'd gawk at him, not able to help yourself, shocked
and thrilled by the sheer, wild mountainscape of him, the way
every bend of joint sets off an avalanche in his sinews. If he walked
into a biker bar, other brawling, burly, surly men would clear him a
path wide as a highway.

That's what I imagined.

It's utter nonsense. Samson was probably average height and
build. He was no more likely to cause a stir by his physical presence than your local high school English teacher. The central
drama of Samson's story is the question, What is the secret of his
great strength?

The *secret* of his great strength.

The Philistine's five rulers were so desperate to know that, that they offered Delilah fifty-five hundred shekels—estimated in today's currency at fifteen million dollars—if she could wheedle it from him.

The source of Samson's great strength was in no way obvious. It was something besides physical prowess, something other than brawn and girth. And it wasn't his hair (an enduring myth that we bald men resent).

It was a secret.

If he had oaken limbs, a Sherman tank of a body, elephantine bigness, who would resort to bribes and threats and extravagant bounties to sleuth it out? Who would break the bank to crack the code? Who would hire, at head-spinning exorbitance, a devil in a red dress to pry it loose?

His strength wore the guise of the ordinary, and its source was not deduced by simple logic. It evaded courtroom cross-examination, backroom interrogations, journalistic grilling. It wasn't spied by the searching eye.

The source of his strength was a secret, and that secret was the Spirit of God.

And, in a way, that was also the secret of his failure.

Samson experienced the Spirit: "The Spirit of the LORD came upon him in power"; "The Spirit of the LORD began to stir him" (Judg. 14:6; 13:25). The Spirit anointed Samson for "ministry." But not once does Samson, as far as we're told, experience or seek the Spirit for more than that. Samson enjoyed and exploited God's empowering presence when he had to perform feats of strength— rend a lion, slay a thousand Philistines, bring the roof down. But Samson had a Philistine inside him—churlish and vulgar, lusty and angry, boorish and foolish—and it never occurred to him to invite the Spirit to conquer that, to slay that, to rend that.

I'm a Baptist, and up until a short while ago we had a doctrine of the Holy Spirit and not much else. We had a theory. We had a creedal position, a theological slant, safely tucked away in some textbook neatly stored away on the high back shelf of some library. Only in recent years have we awakened to the reality that the Spirit of God is a living person, an equal part of the Triune God, who desires to fill us and guide us and teach us and comfort us and counsel us, and to help us bear much fruit.

But he's humble and gentle, the Spirit, and needs inviting. And though the Spirit loves to anoint us for ministry in order to make us God-like in strength, even more he desires to fill us for daily living in order to make us Christlike in humility. More than endowing us with might to slay the Philistines *out there*, the Spirit wants to strengthen us with grace to slay the Philistine *in here*. More than coming upon us in power to rend a lion, the Spirit seeks to lead us into all truth that we might resist the devil, who prowls around like a roaring lion, seeking someone to devour.

Samson embraced the one and shunned the other. He sought the Spirit so that he might be a hero, but never so that he might become a saint. He cried out for the Spirit's power to serve himself, but never to die to himself. Jesus warned about those who perform many miracles—who seemingly have an anointing for ministry—but who bear no fruit (see Matt. 7:17–23).

In the end, Samson's story is tragic. The final note on him, after he pulls down the temple of Dagon on the heads all the Philistine rulers, and buries in the rubble three thousand Philistines and himself besides, is this: "Thus he killed many more when he died than while he lived" (Judg. 16:30).

It's an indictment, not an accolade; a shaming, not a hallowing. In essence, Samson was better dead than alive. He served God's purposes best by getting out of the way.

WE HAVE SEEN HOW CENTRAL AND FOUNDATIONAL FAITH IS IN the life of virtue. If faith doesn't anchor virtue, it drifts, willy-nilly, toward the rocks or the chasm.

But just as vital and indispensable to the life of virtue is the presence of the Spirit. If the Spirit does not stir, fill, and direct both our life of faith and our quest for virtue, all our virtues will grow stunted and bitter, like fruit strained out from hardscrabble ground. Such virtue is usually no more than a repertoire of self-serving gestures.

I know this. I have tried it both ways. It is common to have faith, and even to live virtuously, but to do it absent the Spirit.

The movie *Coach Carter* is the story of Kenneth Carter, who shaped inner-city, ragtag high school basketball players into a tightly disciplined and almost unstoppable team of athletes. Carter inherited a gang and turned out an army. He started with sullen ragamuffins, with no hope for their futures, and in four months ended with steel-eyed warriors and scholars, with dreams for their lives.

To accomplish that, he was brutal. He pushed the boys, always to the edge of their endurance, and then a little further. Any insolence was immediately reprimanded with a crackdown of grueling drills. The slightest lateness was penalized. Backtalk was squelched beneath a mounting regimen of workouts. Under Coach Carter's taskmaster harshness, the boys at first withered, then flourished.

My one comment to my wife after watching it was, "There is no excellence without discipline."

I believe that.

But more and more I believe that there can be no discipline in any sustained way without the Spirit. Discipline can create impressive, even dazzling, results in the short term. But it always needs a

Coach Carter around to prod it and drive it, and after a while that grows wearisome too.

No, the only power on earth that can enliven a whole lifetime of disciplined attentiveness and obedience to God is the Holy Spirit. If virtue's groundwork is faith, its lifeblood is the Spirit.

I think of two men I know, both men of faith and virtue. But one seeks the Spirit and the other doesn't. One invites, daily, the Spirit to meet him and fill him and guide him and empower him. And the other is his own Coach Carter, haranguing himself to work harder, chastening himself when he falls short. In some ways, the second man is more impressive: he is lean and sharp and focused. He gets more done, has fewer mess-ups, can quote, with flawless accuracy, more Scripture.

He just lacks joy. His faith and virtue sour more with each passing year. He struggles with judging others and hating himself, the twin offspring of self-striving. He nurses, I suspect, bitterness toward God. His children are mostly silent, but have watchful, distrustful eyes.

The other man garbles Scripture and can never remember what passage comes from where. He bumbles and ambles at times. He is earthy in a way some people find shocking. He could lose a few pounds, and sometimes forgets, midsentence, what he's talking about.

But he abounds with joy. He gets sweeter by the day. He is one of the few people I know who truly loves sinners and hates sin, and people instantly sense it, sense they are safe with him. His love for God is as inviting as a blue lagoon and contagious as laughter. He is his children's hero.

Some of the difference between these two men is simply owing to temperament. But only some. The one man, the man with joy, was not always like this. There was a time he was angry and self-absorbed, and he nearly divorced his wife. He was a lover of money and a lover of self. But he changed.

And what changed him was the Holy Spirit. This man lives as he breathes the truth of Zechariah 4:6: "'Not by might nor by power, but by my Spirit,' says the LORD Almighty." He pays attention to the Spirit's quiet movements like some men do to stock market fluctuations and others to sports scores. In any situation, he always—well, almost always—sets aside his own gut reaction and asks, "How is the Spirit leading here? What would delight and not grieve or quench the Spirit? In what direction is the Spirit moving?"

Two men, both with faith and virtue. But one of them seeks the Spirit, in season and out. And the other just tries harder.

It's the first one I want to be like.

IN THE CHURCH WHERE I FIRST MET JESUS, I DON'T REMEMBER that we talked much about the Holy Spirit, except to warn each other about the dangers and delusions of *those charismatics*. I remember a lot of fine, upstanding Christians in that church, and a few curmudgeons, stone-faced like rock cod, hard-bitten as exiles. But those are in every church. For the most part, it was a good place to be nurtured in newfound faith.

Looking back, though, I am struck by an absence. There was, as far as I can recall, no extravagance in that church: extravagant joy, extravagant hope, extravagant kindness, extravagant generosity, extravagant grace, extravagant forgiveness. I don't remember any of that. Maybe it was there and I missed it—it was hidden in plain sight—but I think it was rare. What we had instead was prudence. We were a cautious folk, rationing out our money and time and goodwill in small increments. We forgave, up to a point. We gave, up to a tithe. We had faith, as long as the cash was in the bank. We took risks, as long as they were well calculated and we could all be safely home by ten o'clock.

They were good people. I want to emphasize that. They were men and women of faith and virtue, and I learned a lot from them and owe much to them.

But we weren't extravagant.

This might be a skewed way to parse theology, but I think a chief sign of the presence and work of the Holy Spirit is exactly this, this extravagance. Where once we were wary, stingy, reluctant, we find ourselves bighearted, spendthrift, daring. That cold, closed hand of calculation and suspicion, once gripping and tugging us, warms and loosens and then—miracle!—starts nudging us outward. We become simultaneously color-blind and bright-eyed, more discerning but less bigoted. We lose naiveté but gain compassion and will gladly spend ourselves and be spent for the kingdom of God. We actually count it all joy when we go through trials of many kinds. We stop envying others' success and prosperity and start grieving their losses and shortfalls. Our appetite for gossip and blame and self-vindication diminishes, while our hunger for the truth grows ravenous, and with it our desire to strengthen the faltering, praise the mighty, bless the lowly. There's a lightness in our step, a steadiness on our feet, and if we don't dance more, at least we want to.

We become extravagant. Where this quality is absent—where a follower of Jesus is chronically miserly and rigid, stiff-necked and scornful—the Spirit of God is dormant. I know, of course, many happy pagans. I'm not suggesting that they are moved at the impulse of the Holy Spirit. Other touchstones besides this are needed to "test the spirits" and see if they are from God—purity of life, an attitude of servanthood and humility, a devotion to and imitation of Jesus. But where some real and deep manifestation of extravagance is missing in a follower of Jesus, it's a good guess that within that person the Spirit is quenched or grieved, or both.

IN THAT SAME CHURCH—THOUGH HERE I AM QUITE SURE I WAS taught well, but got it wrong anyhow—I never knew any stronger motivation for doing the right thing than guilt or pride: guilt if I was falling short, pride if I was out in the lead. I did not experience the buoyancy and zing of God's pleasure, the weight and sting of his rebuke. I feared, rather, to incur the scorn of church-folk, and hankered after their smiling nodding approval. This had more to do with something in me than something in them. But I particularly recall undertaking a hard regimen of Bible memorization, not because I wanted to hide the Word in my heart that I might not sin against God, but because I wanted to impress my newfound church friends, and this seemed to do the trick.

As anyone who lives this way knows, it's exhausting and embittering. It turns goodness into the mere avoidance of badness. It reduces holiness to a form of hygiene. A few seasons of it made me weary in doing good, and sour as Jonah. At some point I realized that, were I still a pagan, I would never be lured from my waywardness by the prospect of becoming a Christian like myself: a prig and stickler, expert in labeling, blaming, and flaunting my own rightness. I became, in a wink, a whitewashed tomb.

I needed a more excellent way. I needed the way of the Spirit. I can't point to any single moment of epiphany when I changed my mind about this. It was a slow unveiling, a puzzlework of discoveries that took some time to piece together. But the sum of it was the realization that Jesus *lived in me* by his Spirit, and I could live as he did by simply paying attention, listening to his still, small voice, responding to his nudges. And as I attended to the Spirit, I was able to trade in my motivations of guilt and fear for something far more organic and invigorating, a hope, a vision, an invitation. I am still a thousand miles from consistency in this. I still sulk, rant, lust, throw tantrums, tailgate slow drivers. I am overly reckless with my opinions and overly cautious in my convictions. But more and more, it is for the joy set before me that I run the race.

Before I learned the way of the Spirit, I was like a man running with a self-wielded goad sticking in my ribs, a self-dangled carrot bobbing before my eyes. I rigged my own motivations and rewards.

But the Spirit is a wind. I'm learning to run with his gentle pummeling on my back, keeping me from growing weary. Some days, I spread my arms like wings and catch that wind beneath them, and for moments I fly. I fly.

MY FRIEND GARY NELSON IS ONE OF THE BEST PREACHERS I KNOW, but by his own account it wasn't always so. In his greenhorn youth pastor days, when his senior pastor only let him near a pulpit every few months, he preached interminable, ponderous sermons. Assigned a topic, he would exhume every last esoteric detail he could find, assemble them all in factory-line order, and then trot them out one by one. No Greek word was left unturned. No cultural-historical tidbit was omitted. No text, no matter how obscure, no matter how obliquely related to the subject at hand, was neglected.

So on a humid Pentecost Sunday in June, assigned to speak on the Holy Spirit, he spared not the rod. He labored hard at the task: starting with the story of the brooding, sculpting Spirit in the opening verses of Genesis, he began his long march toward Revelation, with lingering stopovers in the Psalms, the Prophets, the Gospel of John. An hour into it the congregation was wilting in the heat, and still he wasn't done. He was, in a way, just beginning. He stepped across the threshold of the book of Acts, nudged up against Acts 2, his Pentecost text. He described the moment: the little band of Christ followers huddled together, praying fervently, joyfully, expectantly. Then a noise, at first faint like distant waves folding on the shore, then like a broom swishing stone. But it gathered until it was like a rushing wind, swift and terrible, bearing down on the room where they met.

"The Spirit hit like a tornado!" Gary cried, and at that very moment every window in the sanctuary shattered, and a wind, swift and terrible, shrieked through the openings.

It *was* a tornado. It skipped, fleet and stealthy, into town while Gary droned on and the congregation slept on. Its great churning funnel was gluttonous for air, swallowing whole landscapes of it, and as it approached it created a vacuum inside the church. When the pressure outside vastly exceeded the pressure inside, the windows popped—the exact moment of Gary's cry of the Spirit.

That got everyone's attention.

The Spirit usually comes to us gentle and quiet. But it's good to remember he is a power huge and elemental, and can make even the dead to wake.

Jesus said, "If you then, though you are evil, know how to give good gifts to your children, how much more will your Father in heaven give the Holy Spirit to those who ask him" (Luke 11:13).

Well, what are you waiting for? Go ahead: ask.

I dare you.

The Petrine Diaries:
If Anyone Speaks . . .

PAUL MET JESUS ON A ROADWAY IN A BLINDSIDE, A BRUSQUE ambush of judgment and salvation. John met him first at the lakeshore, Jesus in the coarse garb of his tradesman life, but encountered him years later in all his cosmic grandeur: towering and robed in dazzling white, sword-wielding and star-juggling, glowing like sun and snow and fire, thundering like a waterfall. It's no surprise then, that it's these two men to whom we owe most of our understanding of the Holy Spirit. They both had vivid, dramatic encounters with the ascended Christ, Christ present in all his Spirit-Otherness.

Peter, on the other hand, knew Jesus best through his flesh-and-blood incarnation. For Peter, Jesus's touch was physical, his voice audible, his breath palpable. The Jesus he knew sweated and slept and ate. His strength flagged. His patience ran thin. He could only be one place at a time, carry on one conversation in any given moment. He liked fish, and afternoon naps, and long walks by himself.

Peter's story is mostly about being with Jesus in the flesh. So we rarely turn to him to learn about Jesus in the Spirit, how Christ becomes real and present to us outside his earthly manifestation.

Which is too bad. Peter has much to say on this matter. Though his direct references are sparse and allusive—he never attempts anything like a creedal or doctrinal statement on the subject—what he does say reveals a rich pneumatology. *The Spirit made Jesus alive*

(1 Pet. 3:18). *The Spirit sanctifies believers* (1 Pet. 1:2). *The Spirit reveals truth to believers and empowers those who speak it* (1 Pet. 1:11–12; 2 Pet. 1:21).

All of this we already knew through the writings of Paul or John or the remarks of Jesus. Peter's unique contribution has to do with emphasis. More than any other writer in Scripture, Peter stresses the Spirit's work and presence in all forms of Christian proclamation—preaching, prophecy, evangelism. For such speech to be more than the spouting of mere words, the Holy Spirit must be poured out upon those who speak, pointing them to hidden things, revealing to them eternal things, carrying them along in strength and wisdom. The Spirit gave the prophets the knowledge of things to come. The Spirit gave the first evangelists the power to speak so that others heard "the wonders of God" in their own language (Acts 2:11). The Spirit now gives preachers the authority to announce the gospel with divine authority.

Peter, I think, must have discovered this the hard way. Much of the public record we have of him portrays a man whose tongue one moment is hair-trigger, the next barrel-tied. He speaks, fluently, words of flattery and treachery, words sprung from cowardice or rashness, honed by calculation. He utters, haltingly, words of confession. His mouth was a breeding ground for outburst and denials. It was a hermitage of taunts and rants and boasts.

And none of it got him what he'd hoped. The opposite, in fact: shame, failure, sorrow. He said things he did not mean and believed things he was too afraid to utter. He spoke with a passion disproportionate to his true intent. He blustered where he should have whispered, stayed silent where he should have ballyhooed.

He was a man of unclean lips who lived among a people of unclean lips, and it awakened in him, though slowly, the cry of woe, and the ache to have those lips burned clean. So it is surprising—or not—that Peter, exhorting his readers about the right use of spiritual gifts, writes, "If anyone speaks, he should do it as one speaking the very words of God" (1 Pet. 4:11).

I am a pastor and a writer. The mouth disease that plagued Peter plagues me. So I have made this my motto—*if anyone speaks, he should do it as one speaking the very words of God*—and I have paid special attention to Peter's teaching on the Spirit's role in this. Especially 1 Peter 1:10–12:

> Concerning this salvation, the prophets, who spoke of the grace that was to come to you, searched intently and with the greatest care, trying to find out the time and circumstances to which the Spirit of Christ in them was pointing when he predicted the sufferings of Christ and the glories that would follow. It was revealed to them that they were not serving themselves but you, when they spoke of the things that now have been told you by those who have preached the gospel to you by the Holy Spirit sent from heaven. Even angels long to look into these things.

Twice here, Peter mentions the Holy Spirit's work in the message of salvation: first, as Christ's presence alive within the prophets, pointing them to the time and circumstances of Christ's suffering and glory, which the Spirit had already predicted through them; second, as the power which enlivens all those who, from the prophets until now, myself included, repeat that message.

Myself included. Those words are breathtaking. On any given Sunday, and other times as well, when I open my mouth to speak of Christ, of his suffering and his glory and the purpose and consequences of these things, I do so by the power of the Holy Spirit—

and if not, without effect. *If anyone speaks, he should do it as one speaking the very words of God.* The thought of it some days nearly paralyzes me in my seat. But on most days, it catapults me from it, simultaneously humbling and emboldening me. Later, when Peter talks about those men who "spoke from God *as they were carried along by the Holy Spirit*" (2 Pet. 1:21; emphasis mine), I know exactly what he means: I have tasted the exhilaration of the Spirit of God catching me up, in all my ganglingness and sluggishness, and giving me an eloquence, clarity, and authority to which I am not naturally born. I could weep with thankfulness and relief. I have spoken so many things in my life that deserve Jesus's severest rebuke—"Get behind me, Satan! You are a stumbling block to me; you do not have in mind the things of God, but the things of men" (Matt.16:23)—that it stuns me afresh with wonder and hope whenever I speak things that win his highest accolade—*Blessed are you, Mark son of Bruce, for by this was not revealed to you by man, but by my Father in heaven* (Matt. 16:17).

Peter had heard, back-to-back, Jesus's accolade and then his rebuke. I'm guessing, having tasted both, more and more he lived to hear the one and avoid the other. And all that stood between the two was one thing: whether he was carried along by the Holy Spirit or just caught up in himself.

The Fisherman's Tale

Call me James. We fished together since we were boys, my brother John and me, and Simon also, and his brother, too, Andrew. My father was a fisherman from way back—my mother used to say he was born in a boat, reeking of fish, and I'm not sure she was joking. Father—his name's Zebedee, in case you were wondering—took John and me out since I don't know when. I remember watching a squall come in, clouds black with rain then white with lightning, lit up like lanterns, and the wind lifting the water overtop us, and my father with a stern look that later I knew was what a man does with his face when his heart's afraid, and him holding the tiller hard and telling us boys to hunker down and grab the gunnels and not let go, and I must have been all of three years old. When I was ten I could handle that boat myself, even in rough water, and cast a net as easy as tossing a stick. And our hands grew calluses hard as tree bark.

Simon was older. He and Andrew had been fishing since before they could remember, too, so when we all got to be men it was the natural thing to do. We didn't know anything else. Sometimes we worked together, other times apart, but we'd all sooner be on water, pulling oars and hauling nets, as anything. Fishing was hard work, sure, and people seemed to avoid you on account of the odor. But you got so you liked that, being left alone. We fished a lot at night, the sky huge with starlight as with laughter, and the lake often smooth and glossy, like the backside of some great beast sleeping. We spent a lot of time waiting. And thinking. And talking, whispering so as not to startle the fish, and because the night seemed to forbid loudness.

We talked about many things—work and women and food and what we'd do if we didn't do this. And we talked about God. Simon especially liked that topic. Did God see us out here? Did he care when a storm came up, or when the fish stayed away? Or did he avoid us, too, like other people did, on account of the odor, on account of our roughness? Was God ever going to show up like he did in the days of Elijah and Elisha, and do amazing things, raise the dead and feed the hungry and cure lepers, and all? Or was that all just for then?

Then Jesus showed up. He showed up in the funniest way, now that I think about it: he wanted us to take him fishing. He'd already met Simon, or Peter, as he liked to call him. After a while we called him that too. Jesus had been guest speaker at Simon's synagogue, and then gone home with him for lunch. He healed Simon's mother-in-law of a fever, Jesus did, and so then half the town showed up at Simon's door, all these sick people you normally stayed away from, and Jesus healed them, too. And he rebuked demons. They came out of people shrieking like shorebirds squalling over fish guts. It was quite a thing, so I'm told.

A few days later Jesus came down to the water, and that's when I met him. As you might imagine, a lot of people were good and curious about him, and so they came down to the water, too, a big crowd of them, hungry for whatever he said. But it got so Jesus was pressed right down to the shoreline, and he stepped into Simon's boat and asked him to push it out a ways, to give him some distance. Then he sat down on that wood bench that Peter had sat on most his life, and he preached. To be honest, I don't remember what he said. We were washing and patching nets, getting them ready for the next night's work, and I was only half listening—I was listening to the voice, not the words, though that can be right powerful in its own way.

Jesus finished with the crowd. But he wasn't finished with us.

He turned to Peter. "Put out into deep water. Let's go fishing."

Peter was none too happy about it. He wanted to go to bed. We all did. We had been at it all night, casting and hauling, moving to this side of the lake and then that side. Every ripple on that dark water we chased like a rumor, every whorl we wondered over like an omen. But all we got were dirty nets. It had rained, too, so we were wet and cold and had misery in our bones.

But we went anyhow. Jesus asked, so what could we do except put our boats out and start rowing? I watched, across the space between us, Peter gather up his net in his big arms like he was lifting grief itself, and then shove it out with a hard thrust of anger. He did know how to set that net down on water as quietly as pulling a blanket over a sleeping child, but that day he lashed the water with it, calculated to spook the fish. He wanted to prove some point, I guess. I could almost read what he was thinking: *What does a preacher know about fishing? He didn't even grow up near water. He was a carpenter, for crying out loud. He might know a thing or two about building boats, but he sure don't know nothing about using 'em. He might know about eating fish, but he's clueless about catching 'em.*

And then, a miracle. Pulling his net, it pulled back. Peter's eyes flew open, and he bent to the task. His arms hardened with effort, and his back and face lacquered up with sweat, and his neck got all tight. He hauled the net against the hull so that the boat listed to the gunnels, and a tumult of fish came teeming up out of the water. The nets started to break, snapping at the knots, and Peter yelled for us to help. He spilled fish into his boat, their heads and tails slapping the keel board, and still there were more, so we took the net and spilled the rest into ours, until both boats were boiling with fish and we were nearly going down from all the weight. Peter laughed then, with a laugh I hadn't heard since we were boys, wild and throaty and full of dreams.

It was good. But then, suddenly, it wasn't. Peter got real quiet. He looked at Jesus, and he got this funny look in his eyes, all stern and worried.

And that's when everything changed. Peter fell down at Jesus's feet and said words I couldn't grasp at the time. "Go away from me, Lord. I am a sinful man."

To this day, I'm not entirely sure what he meant. We were astonished, is the truth of it, and a bit out of our minds. We had waited for a day like this, a catch like this, all our lives. And now it had come, and Peter was turning it into something else. He must have had a notion of something.

"Don't be afraid," Jesus said, speaking to Peter, but he meant all of us. "From now on you will catch men."

And as soon as he said it, we knew he meant right now. He meant for us to choose before we landed, no waiting, no talking. Just decide.

Peter stood up and started tossing fish in the lake. We watched for a moment, then joined him. They hit the water stiff as wood, but after a few seconds they shook their tails, and dove. Those fish sank down in blackness, like fistfuls of silver we had to jettison in a storm.

But afterward, we felt light. Peter stepped ashore and started running.

II

Make Every Effort

5

My Goodness:
Add to Your Faith . . . Goodness

My GOODNESS.

An odd phrase, that, though I use it often enough, exclaiming my own goodness in all kinds of ways: *My goodness, look at the size of that bunion! My goodness, you're tall! My goodness, I'm dizzy! My goodness, I just sped through a speed trap!*

Only, I have no idea what *my* goodness has to do with any of it. I toss about the phrase as mindlessly as I sweat and blink. I suppose somewhere far back in my collective linguistic ancestry those words, their exclamatory force, their incantatory power, were rooted in actual conviction: the belief that *my* own goodness, once claimed and invoked, stood as a hedge against danger, a seal of good fortune. Uttered, they forged a flimsy talisman against life's monumental badness.

My goodness.

In 1908, Ernest Shackleton led the Nimrod Expedition to reach the South Pole in Antarctica. It was a journey of grueling hardship and inhuman endurance. His team, bone-weary and famished, had to turn back less than one hundred miles from their destination. In his diary, Shackleton tells of the moment their food was almost gone, down to a few scraps of hardtack—a bland, dried biscuit. Shackleton distributed it evenly among the men. Some ate it there and then, licking the crumbs off their fingers like starved dogs. Others stored it in their food bags for a time when their hunger became a kind of madness.

That night, Shackleton awoke to a sound. He opened his eyes and, lying still, watched. In the ragged circle of firelight he saw a sight that made his heart sink: his most trusted man opening the sack of the fellow next to him and taking out his food bag.

And then Shackleton saw a sight that made his heart leap: his most trusted man placing his own hardtack into the other man's bag.[1] He wasn't stealing bread. He was sacrificing his own.

My goodness.

Well, not yet.

But I'm working on it.

GOODNESS HAS GROWN DULL. THE WORD ITSELF HAS BECOME so bland, so shapeless, it is almost void, without form. During Bill Clinton's White House sex scandal with his young intern Monica Lewinsky, a countrywide poll was taken in which Americans were asked their thoughts on the president. Most deemed him a "good leader but not a good man."[2] What they meant, I imagine, was that Clinton was competent but corrupt, skillful but deceitful. A man of ability, just not integrity.

Which is bizarre. Is it possible to be a *good* leader and not a *good* man? The Bible doesn't think so. Scripture renders judgment on the kings of Israel and Judea, for instance, on a single touchstone:

moral goodness. Many *competent* leaders—eloquent speech makers, shrewd statesmen, tough militarists, wise economists—Scripture denounces and dismisses because they lacked such goodness. They were idolaters, slave drivers, liars, thieves. Other biblical kings, weak in political or military or economic skill, Scripture praises because they had pure hearts, hearts that sought God.

They were good.

That biblical clarity has gone begging in an age which calls *good* everything from Mother Teresa's legacy to the latest rap star's obscenity. This looseness and vagueness, where one man's goodness is another's folly, plagues our ability to have meaningful conversations about the *good*.

But even if our definition of *goodness* was not so slipshod, so piecemeal, even if it was clear and precise as the word *dog* or *tree*, there's another problem: we seek the good in all the wrong places.

We want to *look* good.

We want to *feel* good.

We even want to *do* good.

God requires we *be* good.

I ASKED SEVERAL PEOPLE TO DEFINE *GOODNESS*. MOST described kind acts: baking cookies for a lonely neighbor, helping a stranger in a pinch, visiting the sick.

Those are wonderful things, no question, and should be done. But all of it is *doing* good, and Peter is talking about *being* good. He is describing a quality of soul that very often results in mercy to the sick, kindness to strangers, hospitality to outsiders, justice for underdogs. But an evil person can do any of that. Hitler's favorite camera pose was with furry animals and little children. Idi Amin used to cry when he heard sad stories. Stalin was kind to his daughters. Even the wicked know how to *do* good.

They just lacked the capacity to *be* good.

The word Peter uses in the Greek is *aretē*. It is often translated as "virtue" and it means "essential, intrinsic goodness." It depicts a goodness that lives in someone even when he's sleeping, even when no one is around to see or benefit from his goodness. It is what a man is in the dark. If Peter wanted to describe *doing* good, he had a perfectly *good* word for doing that: *chrēstotēs*. The gist of that word is "kindness expressed in action."

But Peter chose *aretē*. He chose a word that has primarily to do with something we *are* before it is anything we do, or look, or feel. *Aretē* is the character of God within us, living and active.

And this is not the first time Peter uses the word. He uses it two verses earlier.

His divine power has given us everything we need for life and godliness through our knowledge of him who called us by his own glory and *goodness*. (2 Pet. 1:3; emphasis mine)

By his own . . . goodness. God calls and provides by his own goodness. Out of goodness, God acts. Who God is precedes what God does. His actions derive from his character.

That's implicit in the way Peter pairs goodness with another character trait of God's: glory. It's by God's "own glory and goodness" (1 Pet. 2:9; 2 Pet. 1:3) that you and I are called out of darkness and then lavished with all we need.

When Peter fuses those two divine qualities, glory and goodness, he is, I think, remembering the day Moses argued with God. The account is in Exodus 33 and 34. In that encounter, God threatened to abandon Israel because of her stiff-necked ways, her idolatrous heart and rebellious bent. Moses pleaded with God to remain with the people, and God relented.

Then Moses was bold to ask God, "Now show me your glory."

God responded "I will cause all *my goodness* to pass in front of you, and I will proclaim my name, the LORD, in your presence" (Exod. 33:19a; emphasis mine).

God himself equates his glory with his goodness.

Right after, God calls Moses up the mountain, and this happens:

Then the LORD came down in the cloud and stood there with him and proclaimed his name, the LORD. And he passed in front of Moses, proclaiming, "The LORD, the LORD, the compassionate and gracious God, slow to anger, abounding in love and faithfulness, maintaining love to thousands, and forgiving wickedness, rebellion and sin. Yet he does not leave the guilty unpunished; he punishes the children and their children for the sin of the fathers to the third and fourth generation." (Exod. 34:5–7)

When Peter speaks of God's glory and goodness, I believe he's thinking about this mountaintop encounter between Moses and God. After all, Peter had a strikingly similar encounter. It happened the day Jesus invited him, along with James and John, to climb with him up a high mountain. At mountain's peak, Jesus showed his glory—he transformed into dazzling, unearthly whiteness. Moses and Elijah appeared also and spoke with Jesus, and then the Father spoke over him: "This is my son, whom I love. . . . *Listen to him!*" (Matt. 3:17).

My guess is that, except for the events surrounding Christ's death and resurrection, this was Peter's most indelible, unshakable memory, deep and aching as a war wound, sweet and elegiac as first love. It dismantled and rebuilt most of what he believed about Jesus up to that moment. Both Moses and Peter were given keyhole peeks into heaven. Both were inducted into the company of the God-stricken. Both were vouchsafed glimpses of things unseen.

Peter, in his second letter, recalls that day:

> We did not follow cleverly invented stories when we told you about the power and coming of our Lord Jesus Christ, but we were eye-witnesses of his majesty. For he received honor and glory from God the Father when the voice came to him from the Majestic Glory, saying, "This is my Son, whom I love; with him I am well pleased." We ourselves heard this voice that came from heaven when we were with him on the sacred mountain. (2 Pet. 1:16–18)

Peter, like Moses, was an eyewitness to God's majesty and glory.

And so he knew, just as Moses knew, that God's goodness and his glory are the same thing. He knew that God's glory *is* God's goodness, and God's goodness *is* God's name, and God's name *is* God's character—a God both loving and just.

Goodness and glory are the same thing, two qualities fused into a single attribute. And that single attribute distils into God's name. And the name of God is shorthand for his entire character. God's goodness, thus, is not merely another of God's attributes: it's his very essence, the sum of all he is.

His goodness is his *God*ness.

Add to your faith goodness. It's more than a simple exhortation. It's more than a call to probity and decency and regular hygiene. It is nothing less than an invitation to enter and experience and imitate the very personhood of God—or, as Peter himself says, to "participate in the divine nature" (2 Pet. 1:4).

My goodness.

IN THE GOSPEL STORY OF THE RICH YOUNG RULER, A MAN— a wealthy, pious, decent man—runs up to Jesus (Mark says he fell to his knees) and blurts out, "Good teacher, what must I *do* to inherit eternal life?" Jesus doesn't at first respond to the man's question. Instead—and this is typical of Jesus—he responds to some assumption or motivation he detects beneath his question.

"Why," Jesus asks, "do you call me good?" (Mark 10:17–18).

Matthew records the encounter with a slight but significant variation. "What *good thing*," the man asks, "must I do to get eternal life?"

"Why," Jesus answers there, "do you ask me about *what is* good? There is only One *who is* good" (Matt. 19:16–17; emphasis mine).

Doing good is usually more attractive to us than *being* good. Wanting to know what good thing we must do often strikes us as more urgent, and certainly more manageable, than knowing the one who is good.

Jesus finally answers the man on his own terms. *You want to know what good thing to do? All right . . .* And Jesus gives the man a tedious, intricate, unwieldy list of things to do—pious duties to fulfill, religious feats to accomplish. He gives the man rules for good behavior, a great slag heap of them. The man walks away, sad with defeat.

He can't do it all.

Of course not. Apart from God, no one does good (Rom. 3:12). Apart from God, nothing good lives in us (7:18). Trying to *do* good without first *being* good is doomed to futility.

First, be good. And the only way to be that is to participate in his divine nature—to receive the love of the only one who is good, God alone.

FINE. BUT HOW DO WE MAKE EVERY EFFORT TOWARD THAT? HOW DO we add to our faith goodness?

Three practical suggestions.

First, become a true worshipper. We are not called to be better philanthropists, or better activists, or better therapists, not first at least. We are called to be better worshippers.

It is in loving the Lord our God with all our hearts and souls and minds and strength that we are freed and empowered to love our neighbours as ourselves. In fact, the Greek word for goodness, *aretē*, Peter uses elsewhere:

> But you are a chosen people, a royal priesthood, a holy nation, a people belonging to God, that you may declare the praises of him who called you out of darkness into his wonderful light. (1 Pet. 2:9)

The phrase rendered "the praises of *God*" is *aretē Theos*. It means God's virtue, God's excellency, God's *goodness*.

God in his goodness called you out of darkness. And his purpose was that you, now and forever, might praise him. You might sing anthems to his excellence. He chose you and made you his own, simply because he's good. You fulfill your chosen-ness, your priestliness, your holiness, your peculiarity, through *aretē Theos*, declaring out loud the goodness of God. Peter knows that the more we do that, the more we will live in light and not in darkness. The more we celebrate the goodness of the only one who is good, the more we participate in his very nature.

So worship.

Next, follow the Spirit. The Spirit of Jesus, living in me by faith, cultivates *my* goodness. Paul exhorts us to walk in the Spirit—to be attentive and heedful to what the Spirit is doing and saying. Goodness doesn't need to be pounded into us or coaxed out of us: it springs forth from simply keeping in step with the Spirit (Gal. 5:22–25). Or as Paul says elsewhere:

> Now the Lord is the Spirit, and where the Spirit of the Lord is, there is freedom. And we, who with unveiled faces all reflect the Lord's glory, are being transformed into his likeness with ever-increasing glory, which comes from the Lord, who is the Spirit. (2 Cor. 3:17–18)

We are being transformed into his likeness with ever-increasing glory. Glory and goodness, we saw already, are the same thing: God's name spoken, God's character revealed. So we could just as well say *we are being transformed into his likeness with ever-increasing goodness.* And that transformation, the increase of glory and goodness, comes by living in the Spirit's freedom.

And then, third, find a model. Imitate those who are good. That may sound like it's upending everything else I've already said, but biblical imitation is much more than merely mimicking another's outward gestures. It is impersonating another's inner life, *reproducing* in yourself the motivations of the heart. It's a kind of method acting: mimicking another in order to *become* them. Repeatedly, the Bible calls us to imitate those who live holy lives. "Follow me," Paul often says, "as I follow Christ."

Find a person, or three, who resemble Jesus more than you do. School yourself on them. John makes this explicit:

Dear friend, do not imitate what is evil but what is good. Anyone who does what is good is from God. Anyone who does what is evil has not seen God. (3 John 1:11)

John, of course, is aware that evil people can perform good deeds. But he's talking about people who, in season and out, in harvest and famine, in daylight and darkness, do good because they are good. Only one thing explains such people: they're God-watchers. They've seen his glory.

Become like them.

AT THE FUNERAL OF FRED MITCHELL, FORMER CHAIRMAN OF China Inland Mission, the man who delivered his eulogy said this: "You never caught Fred Mitchell off his guard because he never needed to be on it."[3]

My goodness, is my one prayer.

The Petrine Diaries:
Good for Nothing

I KNOW NOTHING ABOUT PETER'S CHILDHOOD, BUT I'LL HAZARD a guess, because sometimes I think I can glimpse the boy's silhouette beneath the man's frame. Peter had an awkward earnestness about him that he must have picked up early: always the first to volunteer, always wanting to get the right answer, always eager to lend a hand. I imagine him in grade school, a nice enough kid, maybe a bit oafish. A husky boy, clumsy and strong, his hair cropped close to manage its unruliness. He means well but quickly bungles things. He offers to clean chalkboards, but smears them. He jumps up to give answers, but forgets the question.

He wants to be good. He just keeps messing up.

That's all a guess. But this isn't: Peter as an adult had a near obsession for doing the right thing. For doing good. In a funny way, or maybe not so funny, it often led him to do the wrong thing. He blundered where angels feared to tread, literally. We've already looked, twice now, at the transfiguration, but let's revisit that briefly. If ever a man trod holy ground, Peter did then. Jesus, Moses, Elijah—all stood before him, resplendent, and the moment calls for awe. But Peter wants something else. He wants to be useful. He wants to do good. And, praiseworthy as that is, he only makes himself look foolish.

I know this tendency. It's in me, thick and sticky. It's in many of the people with whom I keep company. I'm thinking of a man who used to be around the church a lot, until he ran off with another man's wife and broke up two homes, hers and his own. But almost until the day that happened he was a whirling dervish of good deeds, a do-gooder extraordinaire. There was virtually no task, no matter how messy or menial, he would not stoop to conquer. Everyone, me included, told him he was a good man.

It just wasn't so. He was a man with a heart of darkness. He was a man whose good deeds did not reveal any goodness within, but cloaked a meanness and pettiness and selfishness inside him. Busyness was the whitewash on his tomb.

That's a dramatic example, maybe melodramatic. Most of us are not, to use Jesus's words, wolves in sheep's clothing. Instead we are sheep in sheep dog's clothing, concealing our docility and way-wardness beneath a disguise of master-pleasing eagerness. We look better than we are. Over-performance becomes a subterfuge, a showcase of energy that hides a mother lode of apathy. A display of virtue that is just that, a display.

But at some point we run out of steam for this. If we're deep down lazy, or greedy, or mean, or just bored, sooner or later that breaks through the skin. It's exhausting to keep building the edifice of good behavior on a foundation of sticks.

I think Peter reached that point of exhaustion. And I think I know when: on the lakeshore with Jesus, after the Resurrection. Peter had gone back to fishing. Even though he was eyewitness to the Resurrection, freshly filled with the Holy Spirit, newly com-missioned with a lifelong task of making disciples, he returned to his boat and his nets and his tackle, the things he had instinctual skill for, that his hands knew what to do with even when his mind was far, far away. He may have gone back innocently enough. He probably needed the money: three years of vagrant missionary travels, hustling bread from Samaritans, depending on tricks with fish to feed crowds and pay taxes, had whittled him to bones. He was maybe raw-boned and hollow-eyed. He wanted to stock up. Put some fat on the bones for the lean days ahead.

But I imagine there was at least one other motive: Peter had messed up supremely. His urge to do good and look good had crashed in a tragic way. Peter had promised Jesus he would stick by him no matter what, no matter how many nasty and ugly things were hurled at him. But when the moment of reckoning came, Peter faltered. Once, twice, three times.

Peter went back to the boat, I think, because he was not entirely sure what to do next. He was deadlocked. He'd reached the outer limits of his bravado. He was despondent over the distance between the man he wanted to be and the man he actually was. He felt unworthy and disqualified.

Good for nothing.

Which is often the place, maybe the only place, we learn to be truly good *for nothing*: good, not just when the eye of man is on us, not because we seek the applause of the crowd, not to reap any earthly reward, but only because the God who is good called us out of darkness and into his wonderful light. The good we do then comes from the good we've received. There's no other accounting for it.

There are all manner of good things God wants us do.

But first, he invites us to taste and see that the Lord is good.

And after that, you'll be good *for nothing*.

6

Know-It-All:
Add to Your Faith . . . Knowledge

I'VE BEEN READING JOB AGAIN, THAT EVENSONG OF THE MIS-begotten, that epic poem of the woebegone. It puzzles me almost as much it does Job, how his life shatters with such drastic suddenness. Overnight, ruin overtakes him, happiness flees him, and the locusts devour sevenfold the years that God has blessed him with.

The book that bears his name and tells his story is mostly soliloquies, Job's and those of three companions who show up to comfort him. Only, theirs is cold comfort. They resort to theological browbeating—a barren remedy at the best of times, but utter cruelty for such a time as this. Dogmatics is useful thread for stitching together our patchwork ideas about God. But it's terrible suture for a broken heart.

Job's friends try to "justify the ways of God to man," to use John Milton's lofty phrase. On my count, they do a half-decent job—they're eloquent, orthodox, forthright. They adopt that pulpit tone, favored by preachers for centuries, halfway between scolding and pitying. They *know*, by all appearances. They know, with undaunted confidence and unwavering authority, what this is all about: why catastrophe has befallen Job, what God intends by it and how Job should respond to it. Even Job's wife has a cameo, a brief walk-on part, and she too knows.

But Job, he's not so sure.

He just doesn't know.

At the end, God bursts in, storm-clad and thunder-voiced, and launches into a lengthy, impassioned soliloquy of his own: *Who is this that obscures my plans with words* without knowledge? (Job 38:2). On and on it goes, God drilling and grilling Job with a litany of questions. It amounts to a graduate-level exam in natural history. *Have you comprehended the vast expanse of the earth? Tell me, if you know all this. What is the way to the abode of the light, and where does darkness dwell? . . . Do you* know *when the mountain goats give birth? Do you watch when the doe bears the fawn?* (Job 38:18–19; 39:1)

What do you know?

That is, in effect, God's sole question.

And the answer is, not much. Job and his companions swap opinions. They indulge in speculations. They traffic in assumptions. They trade hunches. But none of them grasps what he sees with his own eyes. They are gloriously oblivious to things right in front of them, the hard datum of the world they inhabit. So how dare any of them suppose they comprehend the world they cannot see?

Bill Bryson's idea to write his magnum opus, *A Short History of Nearly Everything*, began from a single moment of realizing the vastness of his own ignorance. He writes,

> About four or five years ago I was on a long flight across the Pacific, staring idly out the window at moonlit ocean, when it occurred to

me with a certain uncomfortable forcefulness that I didn't know the first thing about the only planet I was ever going to live on. I had no idea, for example, why the oceans were salty but the Great Lakes weren't. Didn't have the faintest idea. I didn't know if the oceans were growing more salty with time or less, and whether ocean salinity levels was something I should be concerned about or not.

And ocean salinity of course represented only the merest sliver of my ignorance. I didn't know what a proton was, or a protein, didn't know a quark from a quasar, didn't understand how geologists could look at a layer of rock on a canyon wall and tell you how old it was, didn't know anything really. . . .

. . . We live in a universe whose age we can't quite compute, surrounded by stars whose distances we don't altogether know, filled with matter we can't identify, operating in conformance with physical laws whose properties we don't truly understand.[1]

What do you know?
Turns out, not much.

MAYBE THE BETTER QUESTION IS, *WHAT DO I NEED TO KNOW?*

Peter writes, "His divine power has given us everything we need for life and godliness through our *knowledge* of him . . . . For this very reason, make every effort to add to your faith goodness; and to goodness, *knowledge*" (2 Pet. 1:3, 5; emphasis mine).

Add to your faith goodness, and to goodness, *knowledge*.

We need knowledge.

But what knowledge do we need? We need to know what we need to know before we can know it.

BEFORE WE GET TO THAT, THOUGH, I WANT TO CONSIDER THE order of Peter's seven virtues. All virtue, we've seen, must be built on faith. Without faith it is impossible to please God. You can add virtues sky-high, but if the foundation of faith is absent or flimsy, the end result is rubble.

Goodness is the first virtue we add to faith. Before the pursuit of knowledge comes the quest for goodness. We saw a chapter ago that goodness, *aretē*, is not initially about *doing* good but about *being* good. It is a quality of soul. The King James Version almost always translates *aretē* as "virtue." In other words, the first virtue is virtue. Ultimately, *aretē* is the essence of God's nature. To grow in goodness is to become Christlike.

That comes before knowledge for the simple reason that knowledge, like the flesh of a puffer fish, has a toxin lurking in it: pride. Knowledge wants to turn us into know-it-alls, to make us show-offs and blowhards and bullies. Those who *know* often want everyone else to know that they know. They showboat their intelligence and flaunt their pedantry. An unspoken but pervasive assumption among many of us is that to know more than others is to be better than they are.

"We know that we all possess knowledge," Paul tells the Corinthians (1 Cor. 8:1). We all know that we know *something*, to some degree, in some capacity. We each, without exception, possess some measure of knowledge. Some know Latin and some pig Latin. Some know how to design motors, others how to fix them, others how to race them, still others how to break them. Some know how to survive a sandstorm, others how to invest in a recession. Some know how to polish stones. Some know how to talk with children.

Good.

But, Paul warns, "Knowledge puffs up" (1 Cor. 8:1).

Knowledge is desirable, but alone it's dangerous. The temptation is to use it as a weapon or a trophy, not a gift. Apart from goodness, knowledge is often wielded to humiliate, intimidate, or alienate others, not for what God intended it to be: a tool to build and bless and serve others. Unless knowledge is laid atop goodness—anchored to it—we grow susceptible to snobbery and smugness.

Goodness detoxifies knowledge. It draws the venom that, consumed in even small doses, can cause alarming swelling of the head. Goodness renders knowledge beneficial rather than impressive.

Smartness is a small accomplishment if you're deficient in goodness. A big head on a small soul is ugly as an orc.

PETER USES THE WORD *KNOWLEDGE* FOUR TIMES IN EIGHT verses. It's the same word each time, with one significant variation. We'll examine the variant in a moment. But for the sake of argument, it's the same word in each instance.

First occurrence, 2 Peter 1:2: "Grace and peace be yours in abundance through the *knowledge* of God and of Jesus our Lord." *Grace* and *peace* come through knowledge. Ignorance, far from being bliss, is graceless and devoid of peace.

The second occurrence of the word is in verse 3: "His divine power has given us everything we need for life and godliness through our *knowledge* of him who called us . . ." Knowledge imparts grace and peace, and it provides *life* and *godliness*—fullness of life, that means, and a deep, unbending commitment to God's ways.

An important word in both these occurrences is the preposition *through*. Grace and peace and life and godliness come *through* knowledge, like starlight comes through darkness, like a river flows through a riverbed, like a rope passes through an eyelet. Knowledge is medium more than substance. It is conduit more than content. Knowledge has little value in itself; it is simply a means by which great treasures get through to us.

The third occurrence of the word is in verse 5. This is the virtue we're looking at in this chapter, and it's also the variant on the word. We'll come back to it a little farther down.

The fourth occurrence of the word is in verse 8: "For if you possess these qualities in increasing measure, they will keep you from being ineffective and unproductive in your *knowledge* of our Lord Jesus Christ."

Knowledge provides grace and peace, life and godliness, and is the key to *effectiveness* and *productivity*. Altogether, then, knowledge is gift-laden, lavishing on us astounding bounty. Without it, we're straining out gnats. But with it, we live in a land of milk and honey, abounding in gifts received and shared.

WHICH IS ALL WELL AND GOOD, ONLY *WHAT IS IT I NEED TO KNOW*?

Simply, *him*. Three times, Peter specifies the object of our knowledge. We are to have "knowledge *of God and of Jesus our Lord* . . . knowledge *of him* . . . knowledge *of our Lord Jesus Christ*" (2 Pet. 1:2–3, 8; emphasis mine).

It's personal. We're to know, not some*thing*, but some*one*.

That begs more clarity. To truly know someone is to know, not just about them, but to know them. I can know all *about* someone— read his biographies, if any exist, tap his FBI file. I can track down his friends, acquaintances, former teachers, lifelong enemies, and pry from them eyewitness reports and tidbits of gossip. But knowing *about* someone is different from *knowing* him. I know a few things about Mel Gibson, but I don't know him. Contrariwise, there are people I know little about but still know.

I've been married twenty-two years. I *know* my wife, Cheryl—and well. But my knowledge of her is not exhaustive, not definitive. There are holes and gaps and deep haunting silences in my knowing. There are hidden within her secrets and surprises still lurking, depths of her history and personality I've yet to excavate. I just learned why, twelve years earlier, she quit her work as a cosmetician. We had a newborn son at home, being cared for most of the week by someone else. Cheryl had to attend a seminar on mascara. Watching a video—a woman's thin, colorless eyelashes thickening, darkening, seemingly lengthening with each miraculous stroke of the tiny spiraled brush—Cheryl had a startling revelation: *she couldn't care less.* Someone else was with her child, the fruit of her womb. He grew and changed, day by day. Soon he would take his first lurching steps and it might not be her arms he tumbled into right then. Soon his babbling would take shape into words, then sentences and it might not be her ears they tickled first. She was stuck in a windowless room watching the festooning of an anonymous eye, and her baby was rapidly approaching manhood.

So she quit.

I never knew that until, just now, she told me.

And yet I know her intimately.

The knowledge Peter speaks about is personal in exactly this way: to know, not just *about* Jesus, but him.

Still, I don't want to overstate this. If we're to know Jesus, we need also to know *about* him. Theology, history, dogma, creed, lore—these are not the same thing as personal knowledge. But they're valuable, even necessary, adjuncts to such knowledge. If I didn't know anything about my wife—didn't know the date of her birthday, was oblivious to her tastes and preferences, was ignorant about her upbringing, indifferent to her hopes for the future—my knowing her would be a flimsy thing, more boast than substance.

Likewise, part of our knowing Christ is knowing about him. The Bible has one word to describe this *knowing about*: *truth*. Truth is the summation and the substance of those things we need to know about. Truth, though always factual, transcends facts. Truth comprises those facts—about God, ourselves, others, the creation—that is the very stuff of reality. To deny or ignore or reject them is to defy reality itself.

What you know about God is either true or not. If it is true, it is a doorway and pathway to knowing him. If it's false, it is a barrier to such knowing, a path leading away from him.

That was the problem with the man who buried his talents (see Matt. 25:24–25). He thought he knew *about* the master—he was a hard man, he thought, a taker and miser. The servant acted according to what he thought he knew.

He was tragically mistaken.

He didn't know the truth. His ignorance *about* the master—his lack of truth—impaired his ability to ever really *know* the master. That's the value of truth: it is a pathway to personal knowledge, to knowing the One who is the Way, the Truth, the Life. When Jesus taught us to pray, "Our Father in heaven," (see Matt. 6:9) he was teaching us to get the facts right, to clearly establish truth—the name, the location, the identity of God. But he never intended we stop there. Truth is only a prelude to intimacy.

Yet the lack of theological knowledge in our day is a travesty and crisis. We're to love God with *all our mind* as well as all our strength and heart and soul. We're under an implicit obligation to learn all we can about God.

In old medieval maps, the cartographer typically inscribed uncharted areas with the words *Terra incognita*, "Unknown earth." A convention then developed to add a warning: *Hic sunt dracones*, "Here be dragons."

Terra incognita was honest. It was an admission of ignorance, an invitation to further exploration. It awakened inquiry. *Hic sunt dracones* was mere speculation, laden with superstition. It was a covering up of ignorance with wild conjecture. It warned off further expeditions. It stifled inquiry. It hid truth beneath a crust of myth making.

This is easy to trip into, not least of all with our God-talk. When our theology is patchy, it's best just to say so, and then set out to fill in the missing pieces. But I find I'm prone to speculate, swap opinions, warn darkly. I'm tempted to cover my ignorance with a flurry of razzamatazz and boondoggling. *Hic sunt dracones*.

Peter, a few verses along, has something to say about such tendencies:

> But there were also false prophets among the people, just as there will be false teachers among you. They will secretly introduce destructive heresies, even denying the sovereign Lord who bought them—bringing swift destruction on themselves. Many will follow their shameful ways and will bring the way of truth into disrepute. In their greed these teachers will exploit you with stories they have made up. Their condemnation has long been hanging over them, and their destruction has not been sleeping. (2 Pet. 2:1–3)

So make every effort to add to your faith knowledge.

AND YET, KNOWING *ABOUT* GOD, NEEDED AS IT IS, IS NO endpoint: it is merely a gateway. The place we want to get to is *knowing* God, which is to say, loving him. "Knowledge puffs up," Paul says. But here's the rest of that passage: "Knowledge puffs up, but love builds up. The man who thinks he knows something does not yet know as he ought to know. But the man who loves God is known by God" (1 Cor. 8:1b–3).

The goal of knowing God is loving God. And then Paul makes this astonishing claim, so sleight of hand it's easy to miss: loving God guarantees that *God knows us*.

God knows us. In the end, that's what matters. God's anthropology matters more than my theology. God's knowledge of me, secured by my love for him, is more crucial, more defining, more determinative, than all the dogmatics I might ingest and digest and regurgitate in a lifetime. God's most terrifying words are, "I never knew you" (Matt. 7:23), just as his most comforting are, "Before I formed you in the womb I knew you" (Jer. 1:5).

Hagar, Sarah's Egyptian handmaiden and mother of Ishmael, discovered that. Sarah—or Sarai, as she was called then—in a torment of jealousy mistreated Hagar, and Hagar, large with child, fled to the desert to die. She chose a waterless death over what Sarai inflicted. But an angel of the Lord met her, hailed her, made promises to her, and sent her back.

She returned with these words: "I have now seen the One who sees me" (Gen. 16:13). That's all she needed: to see the God who sees her, and knows her, and is with her. Knowing that, Hagar found courage—grace and peace—to return to a situation that, before, was beyond enduring.

Knowing we're known mostly comes through love. That's why

the people who are most Christlike are often least professor-like. Love doesn't take immense brain-power—that, in fact, often hinders it. What love requires is a deep soul.

Our church does services at homes for the elderly. I used to dread these: visiting people with scattered minds, ramshackle bodies, root-cellar odors. But then I started to *see* them. Their minds and bodies are ruinous, but their spirits robust. They are men and women who, most of them, can't feed themselves anymore. They've lost bladder control. They don't remember their own children's names. But start singing "How Great Thou Art," and their withered lips open, their filmy eyes brighten, and they sing lustily, every last word.

Such love.

God sees them. He knows them. And though they know little else, they know that.

Paul says,

My purpose is that they may be encouraged in heart and united in love, so that they may have the full riches of complete understanding, in order that they may know the mystery of God, namely, Christ, in whom are hidden all the treasures of wisdom and knowledge. (Col. 2:2–3)

The old saying is true: it's not what you know, it's who you know. Or better: It's who you love, and who loves you.

WHAT EFFORT CAN WE MAKE TO ADD THIS KNOWLEDGE TO OUR faith? I have a few simple suggestions. But first, my counsel is to go slow and steady. There's a curious detail in Peter's word selection.

The word for *knowledge* in 2 Peter 1:5—"For this very reason . . . add to your faith goodness; and to goodness, *knowledge*"—is the Greek *gnosis*. This is the variant I mentioned above. *Gnosis* is a general, generic, one-size-fits-all word for knowledge. It's the knowledge of inquiry and discovery, knowledge that doesn't float down to you but that you reach up to or dig down for.

The Greek word Peter uses in the other three instances is *epignosis*. Same word, just intensified. It means *fullness of knowledge*. Complete understanding. It's *epignosis* that is the channel of grace, peace, life, and godliness and the key to effectiveness and productivity.

In other words, *epignosis*—the fullness of understanding—is attained through an accumulation of *gnosis*. *Epignosis*—total knowing—comes piecemeal, incrementally, bit by bit. You add some today, some tomorrow, some the next day. Over time, that adds up until it becomes the fullness of knowledge.

That *gnosis* that eventually becomes *epignosis* has four main sources.

The first and basic source is Scripture, where we meet God in revelation. The Bible is our primary source of knowledge about the nature and the work of God. Without it, we would be the three proverbial blind men, each of us describing an elephant based on the piece of the animal we happen to be touching at the time. Apart from the Bible we sometimes, in a fumbling way, grasp a truth or two about God, but there's no substance, no coherence, no connectedness to any of it. It's mostly hunches built on guesses. So we look first to Scripture. Like a detective studying photos of a missing person so that we might recognize them anywhere (even if they've grown a beard, lost weight, dyed their hair), become deeply familiar with God's biblical portrait in order to recognize him elsewhere.

The second source is worship and prayer, where we meet God in

Spirit and Truth. God is revealed in Scripture, but not bound there. He's a living God. He speaks to us, moves in our midst, surprises us with himself. The heavens cannot contain him, and the whole earth is filled with his glory. To know God, we start with Scripture and return to Scripture, but he also inhabits our praises. He comes close to those contrite in spirit. He rides on the wind. I have watched many people well versed in God's biblical revelation only really come to *know* him through a worshipful or prayerful encounter with him. They *taste* and *see* that the Lord is good, a truth they never doubted but hadn't experienced. Each time I see this, I think of a scene in *Jurassic Park*, where a palaeontologist, a man who's spent his life digging and dusting dinosaur bones, meets a living dinosaur face-to-face. In that instant, truth becomes real. His knowledge converts into experience, and his life changes with it.

The third source is creation, where we meet God through his handiwork. The heavens proclaim the glory of God, and yet the whole creation groans, waiting for God to finish what he started. Just as you already know something about me—my habits, my preoccupations, my passions—because you have spent time with one of the works of my hands, so we know something about God by spying molecules and peering into galaxies, by watching leaves uncurl and geese migrate and fish leap up the stairwells of a waterfall. Even in the obvious brokenness of creation—the cancer that afflicts our closest friend or the hurricanes that scatter whole cities—we come to know something of God: the one who is mindful of every sparrow that falls, and whose redemption, when complete, will include no less than a new heaven and a new earth.

Our fourth source is community, where we meet God in disguise. In community we work out our love and knowledge of God in earthy and tangible ways, where God often hides among the least of these, or raises up a David, exposing our Saul-like jealousies, calling forth Jonathan-like fidelities. No one can say he loves God, John reminds us, if he doesn't love his brother. We learn, in the mess and the mundaneness of life together, the art of knowing and being known, of loving and being loved. We master the skills for handling all the many wily things that test and twist such knowing and loving.

Scripture. Worship and prayer. Creation. Community. God is hidden in plain sight in all these things.

PETER DENIED THREE TIMES THAT HE EVEN *KNEW* JESUS. A week after that, Christ, dead and then alive, met Peter on the lakeshore. He had only one question for him, though he asked it three times.

"Peter, do you love me?"

"Lord," Peter finally says, hurt, "you *know* all things. You *know* that I love you" (John 21:17).

That is the most marvelous knowledge of all: knowing that the one I love, the one who knows all things, *knows me and knows I love him.*

For Peter, knowing that didn't arrive overnight. It was a slow growth. It was a stumbling, painstaking, zigzagging journey. But he kept adding to his faith *gnosis.*

And one day, he just *knew.*

The Petrine Diaries:
An Ordinary, Uneducated Man

PETER WAS NOT AN EDUCATED MAN. WE KNOW THAT BY circumstantial evidence: he was a fisherman, plying a rough trade, working by hook or by crook. He needed powerful hands with thick rinds of calluses and a grip that could break stones. He needed a mule's back, and a hawk's eyes, and a cat's agility, and a horse's sense.

But he didn't need much else.

He had little time for books, and none at all for empty speculations or idle conversations. Matters that had no immediate bearing on surviving a nor'easter or getting food on the table, tonight, were to him worse than bilge water oozing between the shiplap.

Not that Peter didn't know a lot. He possessed, for sure, a seaman's sixth sense—that twinge in the bones when rain lurked behind a blue sky, that ability to sniff out a storm's scent in a sweet breeze, that capacity to read the water's tautness or roughness as surely as another man reads a newspaper. He knew what it meant when one kind of bird flocked overhead, or when the nets came up teeming with a certain fish, absent another, or when the waves rolled up the beach and left there a dirty tatting of froth. He would know what a dullness instead of a sheen on a fish's belly indicated, whether a seam of dark current was good news or bad.

But he was no scholar.

We know that, too, by an observation that the Sanhedrin made about Peter and his fishing partner, John. The Sanhedrin *were* scholars, scholars all, comprised of men who devoted their lives to the study of scrolls, the weighing of theories, the sifting of history, the stockpiling of theology. They pored over ancient texts, delved into commentaries on those texts. They debated each other on arcane matters, holding emphatic opinions on distinctions so fine nary a hair could split them. Their fingers grew spindly tracing the crabbed and intricate penmanship of scribes. Their faces took on an indelible sternness from all their hard squinting at the dim page.

They were not men whom the likes of Peter and John easily impressed. They were, the fishermen and the scholars, worlds apart. Scholars treasure things fishermen know nothing about, and care even less, just as fishermen relish what men of high culture disdain.

Yet Peter and John astonished the Sanhedrin. Their boldness caught the scholars' attention and set them back on their heels. It commanded their respect:

> When they saw the courage of Peter and John and realized that they were unschooled, ordinary men, they were astonished and they took note that these men had been with Jesus. (Acts 4:13)

Unschooled, ordinary men. Maybe so, but men astonishing in their pluck, their steady-eyed gaze, their unwavering resolve. Most men standing in the presence of the Sanhedrin—Israel's highest ruling council, its Supreme Court, made up of the Who's Who of Jerusalem's society, its cultured elite—would be quail-voiced and trembling, meek and compliant. Perhaps a few would be spitting mad, shouting obscenities, their loathing undisguised.

But Peter and John stood upright and unafraid. They spoke with clearness, boldness, fairness. They didn't bellow, and they didn't quake. They didn't threaten, and they didn't back down to threats. They neither shook their fists, nor shook when others shook theirs. They stood their ground, no more, no less.

And it all had to do with knowledge.

But not just any kind of knowledge. What they knew had nothing to do with what school they'd attended, or their ranking in a graduating class. It could not be measured by SAT scores, IQ ratings, GPA placements. It was not conditioned on the books they'd read, the theories they'd mastered, the officially embossed documents festooning their walls.

It was personal knowledge, having entirely to do with who they knew, deeply and intimately: Jesus. And they knew him by one means only: the slow and ancient rhythm of being with him, in season and out. What one of them, John, would later call *abiding*. They had walked and talked with Jesus, had sat with him in silence, when all words were spent. They had watched him sleep in the midst of a storm, and storm in the midst of their sleepiness. They had seen him angry, weeping, laughing, rebuking, welcoming children, touching lepers, befriending Samaritans.

As theologians, Peter and John still had much to learn. Their own Christology—their ability to articulate in concise language the work and nature of the one they knew—was still primitive, still being forged and hammered into creedal precision.

But they knew Jesus, as friend, as confidant, as teacher, as Lord, as Savior. They knew, as Paul would later put it, the one whom they have believed, and were convinced he was able to guard what they had entrusted to him (see 2 Tim. 1:12). John would later describe such personal knowledge as that "which we have heard, which we have seen with our eyes, which we have looked at and our hands have touched" (1 John 1:1).

They knew Jesus.

You can know, like the Teacher in Ecclesiastes, all there is to know, and find it all meaningless. But to simply know *the one whom you have believed* is astonishing.

Just ask Peter.

7

Get a Grip:
Add to Your Faith . . . Self-Control

THE DAY I GOT MY DRIVER'S LICENSE, TWO WEEKS AFTER MY sixteenth birthday, I crashed my dad's car. The very same day. The car was a two-toned jut-nosed Plymouth, less than a year old, with vinyl upholstery that got sticky as flypaper on a hot day. It was the kind of car businessmen drove in those days, the mid-70s, long and sleek and thirsty, and my dad was proud of it. The day he fetched it new from the lot, he flew along our street with the windows cranked down, his left arm resting on the open sill and his left hand curled over the roof gunnels, his fingers tapping out a beat on the rooftop in time to the radio. The wind knifed through the car's interior so that his comb-over flew from his scalp like tassels. He was a man returning home with the spoils of battle, parading the antlers of a great stag whom he'd outwitted, a beast noble and swift and worthy of the hunt.

He liked that car.

I crashed it.

The entire debacle was my fault. There was another car involved, but not another driver: I spun, too fast, too sharply—too cavalierly—into a parking space at the mall, and caught my dad's car on the edge of the other car's bumper. That bumper skewered my passenger door and then rode my momentum almost to my tailgate. To make it worse, I instinctively threw the car in reverse and immediately redoubled the damage: a gash deep and wide, crooked and ragged and bruised-looking, spanning three panels.

It was a fearful thing, going home to face my father. He handled the whole thing with a mock sternness and, beneath that, grace and humor. But he fretted over how to tell his boss. That car, you see, was not actually his: it was a company car, leased and insured by the people he worked for. The company even covered gas costs and maintenance, and if my dad needed new tires or a new battery in the two-and-a-half years he kept it, the company would pay for that too. And now I had bashed it up—me, a sixteen-year-old kid, my license barely cooled from the printing.

It was unlikely the boss would receive the news with the same grace and humor my father did.

Two days later my dad, alone at the wheel, was stopped at a light when a dump truck driver swerved to miss something and instead hit him. The truck wiped out those same three panels—crushed them like a napkin—and then the driver bolted from the scene of the accident, never to be found. My dad was shaken but uninjured, and to our great joy—mine, I think, more than his—our problem was solved.

The runaway dump truck did it.

But the problem wasn't solved, not really. The problem, I soon realized, was me. My attitude. My irresponsibility. My carelessness and recklessness and foolishness. My runaway arrogance, not a runaway truck driver, was the cause of the damage.

I thought I was in control that day in the mall parking lot. And

the more I thought it, the less true it was. I was, in fact, danger-
ously out of control. What I needed most, what I lacked most, was
self-control.

I had to get a grip on myself.

That was, at this writing, thirty years ago.

I'm still working on it.

PETER'S THIRD VIRTUE IS SELF-CONTROL, AND IT ARRIVES JUST IN
time. Spiritual disciplines tend to have an unintended effect: they
make us proud, in a sly way. Bizarre as it may sound, the very
means by which God intends to teach us humility can produce the
exact opposite condition: an overweening confidence. We start to
congratulate ourselves for having mastered intricate, difficult matters, otherworldly mysteries, surpassingly great revelations. We
become connoisseurs of things unseen. We fancy ourselves special
initiates. It can be a heady experience. We begin to look with pity
and disdain on those poor souls, legion in number, who bumble
along in spiritual atrophy and myopia.

At first glance, being more self-controlled might seem to re-
inforce all these nasty tendencies. Now, on top of goodness and
knowledge, we've added the elegance of restraint. We've put a tight
reign on our tongue, steadied our gaze, become sure-footed. We
don't blurt things out, barge in uninvited, trip over ourselves in rash
attempts to fix everything. We have chastened our impulses and
tamed our desires. We no longer squander our energy or influence
through self-indulgence.

All that—all that serene mastery—can make us proud little
peacocks.

But biblically, self-control is more than merely keeping in check our animal instincts and primitive urges. Its very essence is actually humility, because it has mostly to do with our minds. It is a trained capacity to think clearly about what matters most. It's a disciplined attentiveness to what God has done and is doing. And it is a heightened sensitivity to spiritual reality, including a shrewd awareness of how the devil seeks to play havoc with us. Self-control is really about paying attention. Before it's the strength to hold yourself back, it's the ability to see, without distortion or illusion, what's really going on, and the wisdom to act in light of it.

PETER SPEAKS ABOUT SELF-CONTROL IN HIS FIRST LETTER MORE THAN his second. It's his first letter, in fact, that gives us the framework and interpretive grid to understand his single mention of self-control in his second letter. In the first letter, Peter always pairs self-control with some quality of mind: alertness, clarity, sobermindedness, mental preparedness. You have to be awake and attentive if you're going to be self-controlled—if, indeed, self-control is to serve larger kingdom purposes, not just your own little moral self-improvement project.

And Peter indicates that there are three conditions where we especially need self-control, three contexts in which we better be fully awake, fully engaged, taking the full and true measure of things. In these three situations, self-control determines whether we fail or triumph in kingdom business.

Here's the first.

Therefore, prepare your minds for action; be self-controlled; set your hope fully on the grace to be given you when Jesus Christ is revealed. As obedient children, do not conform to the evil desires you had when you lived in ignorance. But just as he who called you is holy, so be holy in all you do; for it is written: "Be holy, because I am holy." (1 Pet. 1:13–16)

The word that begins this passage is vital: *therefore*. That word hooks us back into the passage that immediately precedes this one, where Peter talks about the great salvation God has bestowed on us. This salvation, the goal of our faith, has been long anticipated: prophets spoke of it, angels yearn for a glimpse of it, the Holy Spirit ignites men to preach it (see vv. 9–12).

Salvation is the name of all you've ever wanted. All your longings, some vague as rumors, some sharp as skewers, are answered in the gift of God's eternal welcome. Whatever you called by other names, sought in other places, hunted by other means, wanted for other ends, was really and always salvation. Salvation feeds your soul's deep craving. Holy men in times past defied kings to proclaim it. Heaven's seraphim and cherubim chafe to peek at it. The Holy Spirit puts in some men fire in the bones to proclaim it.

And it came to your house.

Therefore, be self-controlled.

Be self-controlled? That seems insipid, a paltry response to an audacious gift. It's like saying, "You've just inherited a billion dollars, so stand up straight, keep a sharp look out, and don't forget to floss." It's like being handed an entire country, rich in history, teeming with culture, brimming with wealth, and responding, "That's nice. Do you mind shutting the door—you're letting in a draft." Self-control seems an embarrassingly muted response to the lavish windfall of salvation. If this salvation is what Peter says it is—angel-sought, prophet-told, Spirit-touched—ought we not cartwheel through the streets, sing and reel and jig, dance wild-limbed and sweat-lacquered as David before the ark? Doesn't it call for joyful abandon, not sober-mindedness and self-restraint?

But great victories have been lost through one unguarded moment. Massive inheritances can be squandered through a single rash decision. Staggering gains have been reversed for lack of self-control.

I think of Dale, a man who'd spent a lifetime for something bigger than himself, like the man in Ecclesiastes. He'd tried it all—austerity, debauchery, spirituality. He'd indulged in erotic sprees, dropped mind-bending drugs, sojourned in exotic places, engaged in spine-tingling escapades. He'd made and lost millions. He'd met the Dalai Lama, and prayed in a mosque, and undergone a sweat lodge ceremony with Coast Salish Indians. He'd spent two weeks in solitary stillness on a moon-scoured mountain, chanting Celtic prayers to banish hunger, waiting for the end of all things.

It was all empty.

Then Dale heard the gospel. He'd heard it before, when he was a boy, and even tried it out for a while like borrowed clothes, but it soon seemed to him drab as an old woman's shawl. But this time when he heard it, it went in like fire and water, both burning and soothing.

It changed him inside out. Salvation was the name of all he'd ever hoped for. For weeks and months, he thrilled to it. He gave, spontaneously and vigorously, riveting testimonies of the wreck he was before Jesus found him, the new creation he was now that Jesus had rescued him. He was making plans to be a pastor. He'd met a lovely, godly woman, and they were to be married.

It all went well, until it didn't. Until the adrenaline rush of conversion burned off and Dale became precariously vulnerable to old ways. Somewhere in childhood he'd received a deep wound, and that reopened, reinfected. And so I watched Dale, we all watched him, walk away from the only thing that had ever given him life.

I've seen that story, variations of it, played out dozens of times. Sometimes I see it move in a different but equally tragic direction, where the prodigal son becomes, not prodigal again, but like the older brother, dour, bitter, proud, and very, very religious. But however the story unfolds, much of it can be accounted for by one simple thing: lack of self-control. It derives from a failure to cherish and safeguard the great salvation we've received, and in our carelessness we let other things—vice, heresy, self-righteousness, whatever—walk in and plunder us in broad daylight.

That's why Peter goes on to say that self-control has a clear purpose: to make us holy as God is holy. This virtue does not exist for its own sake. When self-control is not rendered into holiness, it typically wizens into priggishness. It becomes brittle. The aim is otherwise: to make us God-like in purity. To make us holy.

Self-control guards a treasure—God's great salvation. And it produces a jewel—God-like holiness.

HERE'S PETER'S SECOND MENTION OF SELF-CONTROL:

The end of all things is near. Therefore be clear minded and self-controlled so that you can pray. (1 Pet. 4:7)

This world is coming to a close. One day—soon, in God's tabulation of things, though a day is like a thousand years to him and a thousand years like a day—the heavens will shrivel, the earth will scatter, fire will engulf it all, and the world as we know it will be over.

It's nearer than you think. It's nearer than it was yesterday. It's nearer than all our daily rounds and domestic duties distract us from believing.

But it could happen today.

Peter's two letters are largely an attempt to stoke our awareness of what he calls, evoking ancient prophetic imagery, the Day of the Lord. He wants to heighten our anticipation of that day. Peter concludes his second letter with a lengthy, detailed, and vigorous forecasting of it. It will be cataclysmic: blazing fire so hot it melts and consumes the elements themselves, sweeps the heavens empty, scours the earth bare.

And yet, terrible as it is, we're to "look forward to the day of God and speed its coming." For out of the wholesale destruction a new heaven and a new earth emerge (see 2 Pet. 3:10–13).

But first we get ready. We do that by clear-mindedness and *self-control*. And we cultivate such qualities, in this case, for a specific end: so that we can pray.

Which seems, first blush, another anticlimax. The end of all things is near. Every day, it looms closer: a catastrophic end with a glorious outcome. We prepare ourselves, as for any great battle, with clearness of mind, stoutness of heart, steeliness of nerve. We get a grip on ourselves. We stare the thing in the face, undaunted, unflinching. We cheer its coming, and do what we can to hasten its arrival.

And all that for this: to pray.

Not fight. Not preach. Not counsel. Not organize. Not even evangelize.

Just pray.

Well, I know myself. The one thing I'm least inclined to do when all hell breaks loose is to head for the prayer closet. I have other things, many other things, I'm tempted to do first, and most, and instead. In the face of storm, I don't want to storm heaven. I just want to storm about. In the face of impending doom I get so worried and distracted I could make Martha seem like a mystic poet, a contemplative drawn to caves and catacombs. I become my own little tornado of busyness and drivenness. I'm on my toes, swinging wildly, and the last thing I want to be is on my knees.

But what's needed is to pray. And to pray well under such circumstances—when the sky falls, when mountains collapse, when nature's red in tooth and claw—takes exceptional clearness of mind. And enormous self-control.

You have to slow. You have to breathe. You have to stop walking by sight and start walking by faith. You have to willfully set aside, for the moment, the danger right before your eyes in order to bring into focus, vivid and rich, things unseen. You start where all true prayer starts: "Our father who art in heaven, hallowed be thy name . . ." You practice the presence of God, and invoke the kingdom of God, before you worry about where to get daily bread, how to dodge temptation, how to forgive wrongdoers, about who will rescue you from evil.

None of this comes naturally. Our instinct is fight or flight. Our impulse is to panic, flail about, sulk or bolt or holler. The last thing we're *inclined* to do in the face of the end of all things is pray. For that, we need a good firm grip on ourselves.

Of course, this won't happen unless we start now, well before that "great and dreadful day of the LORD comes" (Mal. 4:5). Start now, when maybe the most trouble you face in a day is burned toast, a flat tire, a flu-bug, a few more bills than checks. If in this relative moment of calm, when the bulk of your troubles are domestic (not cosmic) trifles (not tragedies), you cultivate the clear-mindedness and self-control to pray, it will serve you well in the day you need it most. Learn to pray before you react. Before you phone, in a flap, your child's teacher over some alleged mistreatment your child received in the classroom, pray. Before you fly off the handle over another computer glitch, pray. Before you lose heart because of another unexpected car expense, pray. While the most and the worst you have to deal with is a downturn in the economy, a downsizing at the office, a downwind from a poultry farm, pray.

The habit of prayer will not magically arrive for you amid the flaming debris of the apocalypse. You'll have to get it well in hand now, and work it into your daily rounds as patiently as petit point stitches. Then, when that day comes that you need it most, there it is.

To do that, you'll need a clear head.

And self-control.

HERE'S PETER'S THIRD MENTION OF SELF-CONTROL:

> Be self-controlled and alert. Your enemy the devil prowls around
> like a roaring lion looking for someone to devour. (1 Pet. 5:8)

The devil's on the loose. He's hungry, predatory, cunning. He's licking his chops, and the more effective you become for God the more delectable you look to the devil. He likes a fruitful Christian as much as God does, but for very different reasons: God, to delight in; the devil, to devour.

The devil never got so busy as when Jesus stepped into ministry. Those were bustling days for Beelzebub, staging showdowns in deserts, sending his henchmen scurrying about the countryside to torment children and stir up mobs. It all had a frantic, patched-together, last-ditch feel to it, a petty warlord besieged in his little bastion and resorting to stuffing the canons with tableware and flinging out the contents of bedpans over the ramparts.

Lord of the flies, indeed.

But he was busy. He was giving it his best, worst shot. The Son of God had come personally, preaching and ushering in the kingdom, healing, redeeming, attending to eternal things. And it made the devil angry. It made him hungry. He just wanted to chew something up, swallow it down, spit out the bones.

Jesus promised us that we would do even greater things than he did. He reached a few. We've reached millions. He healed the sick. We've healed whole communities, sometimes entire nations. He walked on water to cross to the other side. We fly through the air, and go to places in a single day once too remote and difficult to reach in a year of trying. He preached in Galilee and Jerusalem. We've preached, nearly, to the ends of the earth.

It just makes the devil angry. It makes him hungry.

So he prowls. He looks for someone with their guard down—not paying attention, getting a little sloppy—and he pounces.

What's called for is, again, clear-mindedness—alertness. And self-control. Don't give the devil a foothold. Don't give him a leg to stand on. Don't turn your back on him: he may seem a mangy hobbling old lion, arthritic and droopy-skinned, only a sad parody of Aslan, but he still knows a trick or two and can move blinding fast in short bursts.

On one of my trips to Africa I spent some time in the grasslands, among skittish wildebeests and wary zebras, sprinting gazelles, lumbering elephants, loping giraffes. It was all very lovely. But most entrancing were the lions. The thrill of coming upon a pride of them, stretched out lazy among outcrops of rock, drowsing beneath scraggly thornbush, never dimmed. I could watch for hours.

One day we came upon a lone lion, a male, hulking and pacing. His mane was brambly, dark at the roots. He was on his feet, restless, his great girth borne like Cain's curse. Not stalking, but looking for something. Prowling. As we came close to him, he stopped, he turned. He glowered at us and bared his teeth. His yellow eyes burned with menace and loathing.

I remembered a movie I had seen a few years earlier: *The Ghost and the Darkness*, about the man-eating lions of Tsavo, a park a few hundred miles from where I was now. Those two lions—true story—terrorized the workers in the 1800s who were pounding in a railway line from Nairobi to Mombasa on the Gold Coast. They devoured many men. They were capricious, those lions, devious and ingenious, more hungry to kill than to eat.

Was this an offspring? His manner—solitary rather than companionable, surly rather than aloof, restless rather than resting, prowling rather than lounging—was different from all the other lions I'd seen. I started to worry. We were in an open-sided Jeep. We were mere feet away. He looked weary and sore—our guide thought he might be sick or wounded—but capable of swift, massive violence. I remembered from the movie a scene where one of the lions leaps through the air, its huge body eclipsing daylight, descending to earth like a terrible prehistoric bird of prey to crush and rend its victim.

The devil prowls like a roaring lion, seeking someone to devour.

The best defense is resistance. If you turn and run, he'll only give chase, and soon overtake you. You have to stand him down, outflank him. You have to do what those of us who live close to mountain wilderness are told to do if we meet a cougar: face him and stretch out as big as you can—on your toes, arms thrust skyward—and shout like a warrior charging.

And what best prepares us for such resistance is alertness and self-control. That's what allows us to *stand firm in* our faith (v. 9).

At a conference I attended a couple of years ago, a speaker named Jack Groppel told about a corporate training center he runs in the Florida Glades. At it, they put new participants through a kind of skills and endurance test their first day. They form the participants into two teams and give them their mission: to run a trail through the forest to the property's perimeter, grab a flag tied to the fence, and run back. But beware, they tell participants: the terrain is treacherous. Venomous snakes, swampy bogs, stinging plants, the occasional crocodile. And one more thing: a wild boar has been spotted in the area. These beasts are vicious, unpredictable, territorial, easily provoked.

Ready? Go!

Jack had a cameraman crouched and camouflaged in the bushes a short way down the trail. His job was to capture on film the team as they rounded a corner. When the team was a few feet off, he was to rustle the bushes and make angry grunting sounds, all the while keeping the camera eye on the team members to register their reactions.

The first clip was of a group of professional football linebackers. Big men, meaty and surly-looking, pushing three hundred pounds each, with thick arms and thicker legs like trunks, and midriffs like oak barrels. They rounded the bend—looking skittish, eyes darting back and forth. They got within the set distance. The bushes rustled. The grunts sounded.

To a man, they flew into wild panic, turned tail, and ran. They abandoned, abruptly and ignominiously, their mission.

The second clip was of a group of CIA operatives. Lean men,

taut and agile. They rounded the bend, looking alert. They got within the set distance. The bushes rustled. The grunts sounded.

To a man, they turned, faced the threat, and instinctively took up combat position. They stood firm in their mission.[1]

They were clear-minded. They were self-controlled.

That's what Peter is asking us to cultivate in order to stand firm in our faith. In the face of an enemy attack, the first thing we often shuck is faith—the very foundation we talked about in chapter 2. We don't stand firm in it: we just dump it and go. Faith is what we need most at such moments, and what we're in danger of losing first.

But to do otherwise takes self-control.

Peter adds one more incentive to cultivating self-control: "because you know that your brothers throughout the world are undergoing the same kind of sufferings" (1 Pet. 5:9).

Every follower of Jesus goes through this. You're not alone, and it's not about you. This is commonplace. This is standard issue. This skill and endurance test is administered to all participants, no exemptions. You have not been uniquely singled out for suffering, as though you were specially cursed or specially favored, as though God likes you less or more than anyone else. This is just what the people of God must deal with.

But you do stand with a great cloud of witnesses, with men and women all over the earth—in Guatemala, in Sweden, in Vietnam, in Sudan, in Angola, in Iraq, in Pakistan, in Japan, everywhere—who are going through this very same trial.

The ones who pay attention, who get a grip on themselves, pass the test, always. They stand firm in their faith.

Be like them, self-controlled.

Because of the greatness of the salvation you've received—and that you might be holy.

Because the end of all things is near—and that you might pray.

Because your enemy the devil wants to eat you alive—and that you might resist him.

And, between now and then, it just might keep you from crashing the car.

The Petrine Diaries:
The Devil's Schemes

PETER HAD A CERTAIN INTIMACY WITH SATAN. I DON'T KNOW how else to put it. God-fearing though he was, he was susceptible as Simple Simon to Satan's wiles and snares. He kept setting himself up as Beelzebub's plaything, his errand boy. What comes to mind immediately is his famous blunder just after he confessed Jesus as Messiah and received from Jesus almost unbounded authority. Jesus began to tell his disciples about his betrayal, the mock trial, the bloody death he was to go through.

> Peter took [Jesus] aside and began to rebuke him. "Never, Lord!" he said. "This shall never happen to you!" (Matt. 16:22)

Freshly endowed with heaven's authority, Peter straight off launches into his first Act of Parliament, binding on earth what, in his mind, is bound in heaven: the terms of Messiahhood. No nails. No blood. No crosses. Peter envisions a clear, clean, uninterrupted campaign that will sweep Jesus from wandering storyteller and itinerant wonder-worker to exalted and triumphant ruler—from the woodshop to the throne room with no further delays, his enemies sacked and bundled into a footstool for him. There's no room for crucifixion on Peter's road to victory.

"Get behind me, Satan!" is Jesus's response to this.

As the apostle Paul would one day explain to Timothy, there are otherwise good, God-honoring people who, for one reason or another, fall into the "trap of the devil, who has taken them captive to do his will" (2 Tim. 2:26). They're as easy prey as rustics at a carnival.

Peter fell into that trap more than once. At the Last Supper, Jesus warns him, "Simon, Simon, Satan has asked to sift you as wheat. But I have prayed for you, Simon, that your faith may not fail. And when you have turned back, strengthen your brothers" (Luke 22:31–32). Peter, who now accepts Jesus's terms of Messiahhood—the shadowy, messy, bloody nature of it—nevertheless and yet again protests Jesus's version of how things must unfold. Jesus predicts that his followers will scatter. Peter thinks otherwise, at least in his case. "Lord," he says, "I am ready to go with you to prison and to death" (Luke 22:33).

Before, in the matter of Christ's suffering and death, Peter opposed Jesus, and Jesus rebuked him for taking Satan's side. Now, in the matter of Christ's suffering and death, Peter supports Jesus, and wants to show him how far outside Satan's camp he's traveled: not only will he make no attempt to prevent Christ's suffering and death—he'll join him in it. He'll jump right in. If he couldn't be campaign manager for Jesus's meteoric rise to grandeur, he'll be his one true boon companion in his darkest, meanest, loneliest hour. They can be suffering servants together.

Jesus this time doesn't rebuke Peter—he just skewers his pretensions: "I tell you, Peter, before the rooster crows today, you will deny three times that you know me" (Luke 22:34). His tone, I think, is weary and sad.

Peter falls silent. And, as Jesus forecast, the next few hours reveal a man, not noble-hearted and heroic, scoffing at danger, but faint-hearted and cowering, begging for shelter.

Satan sifts Peter like wheat. Threshed. Thrashed. Winnowed. Shorn hard of husks. Pounded free of chaff. All things that can be shaken are shaken, fiercely and mercilessly, laid bare to the wind and carried off in gusts that pummel and twist. The man left sprawled on the threshing floor is not the proud, tall stalk of a prince we met before. He is a man reduced to a fistful of seed, each small as a child's tear, ready to be hidden in the earth or crushed beneath the grindstone: to be humbled, slowly, into usefulness.

Sifting is never pleasant at the moment. The one who holds the winnowing fork, we behold in horror, is horned and clawed, doing his best to do his worst.

But here's the holy irony: what the devil means for evil, God uses for good. Did Satan actually ask to *sift* Peter like *wheat*? Were those his words? Did he come to the throne room, as he does in Job's case, and request a lifting of all protective shields around Peter? And if so, did he couch his request in these agricultural terms—sifting, threshing winnowing, separating wheat from chaff?

Or is that the way God outwits the devil's schemes—takes what Satan intends for our ruin and turns it into a means for our strengthening? Did Satan ask to *destroy* Peter, plain and simple, without ambiguity, free of metaphor or euphemism? Whatever he asked, God said yes. But the devil never seems to know the deeper magic.[2] He seems always to miss the fact that suffering is God's crucible for sainthood. Demonic ruthlessness God subverts into a refiner's fire.

Sift you like wheat. Maybe those were Jesus's words, then—his way of recasting reality, of explaining to Peter that the devil, himself blind with pride, had overreached himself, and that his own triumph would be his defeat. It wouldn't be the first time that had happened. It wouldn't be the last. What the devil uses to shatter us,

God uses to purify us. Not only will Peter survive this, Jesus is saying, but he will become a gift to others through it.

The devil has nothing to gain here. Did he know that all along, or was this God's sting operation, the weapon God tampered with so that it backfired in the devil's face?

We don't know.

We do know that Peter, indeed, grew stronger. His faith did not fail. He was not ruined, but deepened. And he did turn back to strengthen his brothers. More than that, he turned back and led them.

But part of what he learned was to beware the devil's schemes. He learned to espy, a long way off, Satan's trap, and go around it. And except for one later incident,[3] it appears Peter was never again outwitted by the devil.

The old serpent can shape-shift into a lion, not whispering but roaring, not tempting us to eat, but tempted to eat us. But sometimes, he just looks for someone to sift. Peter had been on the brunt of that more than once, and learned its hard but valuable lessons.

He got a grip on himself. He got clear-minded and self-controlled, and ever after Beelzebub fled his coming.

8

Too Soon to Quit:
Add to Your Faith . . . Perseverance

GRACIE ALLEN, A ONE-TIME VAUDEVILLE ACTRESS AND THE wife of George Burns, wisecracked and slapsticked her way into America's heart. She was a comic both on and off the air, famous for her pranks and practical jokes. Sometimes people returned in kind. One day a parcel from a friend arrived, special delivery. Inside wasn't a pair of silk gloves or a ruby-crusted brooch or a jeweled hairpin from Park Avenue. Inside was a baby alligator, wriggling and snapping, but still too small to do much harm.

Gracie was heading out the door at the moment. She was flustered about what to do with the little carnivore. So she put it in the bathtub, walked out the door, and forgot about it completely.

When she arrived back home, she found a note on the counter. It was from her maid. It read,

Dear Mrs. Allen,

I quit. I don't work in no house with an alligator. I should have told you this when I started. I just never thought it would come up.[1]

I'm guessing that you've been thinking about quitting, too, and for pretty much the same cause: you don't work in no house, no job, no church, no marriage, with an alligator. You're weary to death from praying for someone who, it seems, will never change—in fact, who's more oafish and mulish than ever. You've tried to take every thought captive and make it obedient to Jesus in a work environment that daily bludgeons you, or worse: that seduces you, inch by inch, into cynicism and gossip and sexual innuendo. You've endured now for the better part of a decade a church that, every time it's about to get serious about worship and prayer and outreach, erupts into another squabble over some minor point of doctrine.

You just want to quit. You don't work in no place with an alligator.

Or maybe you want to quit what you've already quit—you quit drinking, but you crave for just one more teensy-weensy little mouthful. You quit smoking, but you're foul-tempered and jangle-nerved and have pretty much convinced yourself you picked the wrong month to do this. You quit pornography, but you're having this argument with yourself that the problem wasn't all that bad, and one last peek won't hurt. You've quit gossiping, but this latest news is an outrage, and you feel a moral obligation to pass it on.

It's hard to work in a house with an alligator.

Peter understands.

For this very reason, make every effort to add to your faith . . . perseverance. (2 Pet. 1:5, 6)

Add to your faith goodness, he says, and to goodness knowledge, and to knowledge self-control, and to self-control . . . perseverance.

Don't quit, he's saying. It's too soon to quit.

The word Peter uses for *perseverance* is *hypomonē*. Literally, stand your ground. Maintain your position. Stick to your guns. Don't let setbacks defeat you. *Hypomonē* was mostly a military term used to describe a soldier holding position. There were, there always have been, two primary conditions in which enlisted men wrestle the temptation to abandon post: when nothing's happening and the days stretch on and on in dreary tedium, and when all hell breaks loose and each moment rains down terror.

Either way, stand your ground.

Alligators or not, it's too soon to quit.

PETER EXHORTED US TO BE GOOD. THEN HE ENCOURAGED US TO have knowledge. Then he admonished us to be self-controlled. Now he reaches the midpoint of his seven virtues.

We're halfway there.

But halfway is only halfway. We've traveled a good distance, yes. But there's a long journey still ahead.

And the initial euphoria has burned off. The sense of elation and expectancy we had starting the journey dissipated a while back, under the gathering weight of blisters and sore muscles and aching bones. It's getting lonely and hard, this God-walk, an alternation of drudgery and mayhem, the doldrums relieved only by ambushes. Weariness accumulates. Our sometimes heroic efforts have produced measly results. Are we actually getting anywhere?

The growing temptation is to desert, to abandon the operation altogether.

It's at that moment Peter says, *Don't quit. It's too soon to quit. Stand your ground. Stay put.*

Persevere.

He's writing to people with a cartload of reasons to quit. These people were having not just a bad day, but a bad decade, or two. They met with alligators at every turn. Some of this badness was due to life itself: the usual round of upsets and hardships, sicknesses and setbacks. The sheer brokenness of creation.

But most of it was owing to one thing: *they had said yes to God.* They were Christians at a time when—and a place where—that was a dangerous and costly thing to be, foolhardy even. Townsfolk were suspicious and hostile toward them—these peculiar people, cannibals maybe, eating the flesh and blood of their leader, who refused to honor the local deities and so must be the cause of last spring's drought or this fall's blight. They were, these Christians, a soft, wide target on which to pin cosmic blame. Peter mentions suffering seventeen times in his first letter alone. It is, in fact, the grand theme of that letter. The suffering he describes, most of it, would vanish immediately if these people did one simple thing.

Quit.

Quit your faith, or at least quit talking about it. Quit obeying God, especially when it puts you at odds with what everybody else is doing. Quit worshipping. Quit walking in purity. Quit believing Jesus is coming back. Just quit, and the pain will go away. Say, "I never knew him," and everyone will leave you alone.

Isn't that right, Peter?

But Peter's been made wise through his own failings and sufferings. And so he's adamant: "Don't quit. Trust me on this one."

One of the earliest and most defining battles of the American Civil War was at Shiloh. The Confederates generally anticipated that they were going to win the entire war at that one engagement, and the first day seemed to prove them right. They so overwhelmed and pounded the Union forces that by nightfall it looked as though the Union's only option was full retreat and, perhaps, complete surrender. The Union's chief military engineer James B. McPherson came to the Union general Ulysses S. Grant. "Things look bad, General," he said. "We've lost half our artillery and a third of the infantry. Our line is broken, and we're pushed back nearly to the river."

Grant listened but remained silent.

McPherson waited, and then asked, "General, what do you intend to do?"

"Do? Reform the lines and attack at daybreak. Won't they be surprised!"

And they did, and they were. The Union snatched victory from the Confederates and three years later won the war.[2]

It was too soon to quit.

PETER'S TWO LETTERS LIST AT LEAST A DOZEN REASONS THESE Christians would want to quit.

- They live like refugees, like strangers in the world, scattered throughout the earth (1 Pet. 1:1).

- They "suffer grief in all kinds of trials" (1 Pet. 1:6).

- They are falsely accused, blamed for things they never did (1 Pet. 2:12).

- They are subjected to brutal working conditions (1 Pet. 2:18–19).

- They are punished for doing good (1 Pet. 3:13ff).

- They are enticed to sin by those around them (1 Pet. 4:3).

- They are abused and insulted when they won't join the sin of others (1 Pet. 4:4).

- They are punished for following Jesus (1 Pet. 4:12).

- They are harassed and threatened by the devil himself, who wants to eat them alive (1 Pet. 5:8ff).

- They are surrounded by false teachers trying to mislead them (2 Pet. 2).

- They are mocked by neighbors who find their faith naive and deluded (2 Pet. 3:3ff).

- They are disappointed with God, who seems to be slow in keeping his promises (2 Pet. 3:9ff).

Following Jesus has not been a great career move. It has not enhanced reputations and expanded opportunities. It has not made anyone rich, or popular, or influential. It's had the opposite effect: it's turned these people into oddities and outsiders, objects of ridicule, lightning rods of suspicion, targets of abuse. Peculiar people, indeed. It's made their work harder. It's strained their relationships with family, old friends, work colleagues, the boss, the government. They've become everyone's favorite whipping boys and scapegoats. People don't talk behind their backs: they mock them to their faces.

Just quit. It's easy. Throw in the towel. Admit defeat. You made a mistake. You backed the wrong party.

Why keep at this if it's wrecking your life?

Because it's the one thing saving your life.

The most obvious and most overlooked thing about perseverance is that it only makes sense if you're heading in the right direction. If you're not, you're a fool to persist. If you are, you're a fool to quit, no matter how hard the journey. If you have found the one road that leads to life, stay the course. The Bible often compares the Christian life to a race or a battle. Those are good metaphors, not only because they are honest depictions of how bloody and grueling it can be, but because both races and battles have this in common: the point is to win. There is a goal before you. This is not random struggle. This is not suffering for its own sake. Either this accomplishes something worthwhile, or don't bother.

The movie *Rabbit-Proof Fence* is the true story of three girls in Australia—sisters Molly and Daisy, and their cousin, Gracie—who in 1931, were torn from their home and literally from the arms of their grandmother and taken twelve hundred miles away to be placed in a residential school. The girls were half-castes, part Aboriginal, part white. The law in Australia was similar to the law in Canada at that time: forcibly remove these children from their families and communities and educate them under conditions of brutality, abuse, shame, and deprivation.

The three girls escape. But the only way they know how to get home is to follow a rabbit fence, a fifteen-hundred-mile wire mesh fence that snakes along the wilds of western Australia. It is a journey of Homeric proportions. They trudge through blistering desert, evading wild animals, trackers, police, surviving on food they scavenge. They return, nine months out, to a joyful reunion with family.

Years later, one of the girls, Molly, now a mother and pregnant, is again taken captive and returned to the same school. She escapes once more, this time with her children. She makes the journey all over again, under harder constraints.

A journey that dangerous and difficult, that long and arduous, only makes sense if the road leads home. As old ladies, Molly and Daisy reflect on their life, and decide that they would do anything, they'd do it all over again, just to get home.[3]

If you're walking toward nothing or fighting for no clear purpose, then quit.

But if the road leads home, never give up. Churchill rallied the people of Britain in their fear and discouragement, rubble up to their ears, to never surrender. He saw the goal. He kept in focus the finish line. He inspired an entire nation to persevere, not because suffering had any value in itself, but because they were on the only road home.

That's what Peter does. Stay the course, he says, because of what is ahead—the glory that will be revealed:

> Concerning this salvation, the prophets, who spoke of the grace that was to come to you, searched intently and with the greatest care, trying to find out the time and circumstances to which the Spirit of Christ in them was pointing when he predicted the sufferings of Christ *and the glories that would follow*. . . . I appeal as a fellow elder, a witness of Christ's sufferings and one who also will *share in the glory to be revealed . . . you will receive a rich welcome into the eternal kingdom of our Lord and Savior Jesus Christ*. . . . You ought to live holy and godly lives as *you look forward to the day of God* and speed its coming. That day will bring about the destruction of the heavens by fire, and the elements will melt in the heat. But in keeping with his promise *we are looking forward to a new heaven and a new earth, the home of righteousness*. (1 Pet. 1:10–11; 5:1; 2 Pet. 1:11; 3:11b–13; emphasis mine)

Peter has the ultimate end in view. He has his eye on the prize. He virtually cannot speak of suffering without also speaking about the magnificent reward on the other side of suffering. In that, he is like the writer of Hebrews, who described Jesus's willingness to endure the cross—to persevere—inspired by the joy set before him. As Christians, we are not taught to enjoy pain: we're taught to endure it for the sake of a joy that will, with one taste, banish even the memory of what we had to go through to find it.

I have in my years of being a pastor talked with many people who want to quit, or to quit what they've quit. My approach with them is pretty much the same every time: Where did you think this road was leading? If it's no place you want to get to, then quit, by all means. Don't let me talk you out of it.

But what if this is the only road home?

Peter had that revelation early in his sojourn with Jesus. Jesus multiplied bread and fish for five thousand hungry people who had followed him out into the wilderness. Jesus knew how to throw a festival, a happy convivial gathering, with upbeat praise music and Starbucks coffee and French pastries. He knew how to draw a crowd.

And then Jesus turned around and sabotaged it. His next sermon series was churlish and grisly, with gruesome illustrations, and it emptied the pews. He scolded people for wanting more bread. And he told them the only way to have life was to get real food: to eat his flesh, to drink his blood. That conjured images at once too cryptic and too graphic for most of his listeners, and "from this time many of his disciples turned back and no longer followed him" (John 6:66).

Jesus seems unfazed. He simply turns to the original Twelve and asks, "You do not want to leave too, do you?"

It's Peter who's ready with an answer: "Lord, to whom shall we go? You have the words of eternal life. We believe and know that you are the Holy One of God" (John 6:68–69).

We're on the only road home.

We'll stay the course.

THE MOST SIGNIFICANT THING PETER DOES TO HELP US HERE IS provide a theology of suffering. His argument is finely textured and many-layered, but the sum of it is this: Christianity does not provide a supernatural cure for suffering; it provides, to use A. J. Conyer's crisp phrase, a supernatural use of it.[4] God doesn't magically dispel suffering, at least not most times: he enters into the thick of it and uses it to accomplish something in us, and often through us, that no amount of pleasure or success could ever produce.

Peter enumerates some of the values God conjures from our suffering:

- It refines our faith (1 Pet. 1:6–7).
- It perfects our hope (1 Pet. 1:8–9; 1:21).
- It weans us from sin (1 Pet. 4:1–3).
- It deepens our intimacy with Jesus (1 Pet. 4:12–13).
- It trains us in holiness (1 Pet. 4:16–19).

It's entirely possible, of course, that suffering will produce the exact opposite effects: corrode our faith, shatter our hope, estrange us from Jesus, provoke us to rebellion, plunge us into sin. The difference is simply this: Do you believe that you are on the right path, or not? Do you believe that, though the whole world teems with alligators, this is the one road home?

If you believe you are, stay the course.

THIS MAY BE A GOOD NEWS—BAD NEWS MESSAGE FOR YOU. THE good news is that God has holy purposes in your suffering, no matter the shape and cause and depth and duration of that suffering. The bad news is, as much as you want God to save you out of the suffering, he might have other ideas. God is more intent in helping you to work out your salvation *in and through* the suffering than he is in whisking you out of it.

Only, you'll need to persevere.

How?

Faith.

That's the place we began. Faith is the substance of things we hope for but have not yet seen. "Though you have not seen him," Peter says, "you love him; and even though you do not see him now, you believe in him" (1 Pet. 1:8). Faith is the firm belief that God exists—he hasn't abandoned you—and that he rewards those who earnestly seek him—he's not out to get you.

But he is out to perfect you.

Suffering hands us a unique opportunity to refine faith. It's an opportunity, not to lower our expectations, but to redefine them. What were you hoping for? A better house? A better job? More money? A slimmer figure?

Is that it?

Suffering teaches us to hope for something that nothing in this world can deliver, to look forward to something so big, so bright, so wild, so audacious, the world can't contain it.

When faith has shown you the only path home, the only place you really want to go, you stay the course.

NATAN SHARANSKY WAS A COLD WAR PRISONER, A REFUSENIK of the old Soviet Empire. He was a thorn in the Soviet's side, and they did with him what they did so often—with mindless repetition, numbing frequency, icelike rigidity: put him in the Gulag and left him to rot.

But Sharansky had friends on the outside, lots of them, who wouldn't shut up. They created an international ruckus, and finally the Soviets decided it was easier to be rid of the man than to keep him. The moment of his release came on a wintry day in February 1986. The Soviets brought him into what was then Communist-controlled East Germany, to the Glienecke Bridge, which linked the two halves of Berlin. On the eastern side stood Sharansky, in a huddle of Soviet officials. On the west swarmed a massive crowd of press and friends and family, well-wishers and onlookers. Finally, to the cheers of everyone on the western bank, Sharansky was released. He walked unaccompanied across the bridge.

But he did a strange thing. He zigzagged. He skipped, and dallied, and cantered, and danced.

He took his time.

He reached the other side to a thunderous welcome. In a moment of lull, he explained himself: "The KGB told me to cross in a straight line, and you know I never make an agreement with the KGB."[5]

There's a voice inside you, I'm guessing, menacing and insistent, telling you what to do, telling you to quit: just walk straight there and get it over with.

Don't make an agreement with that voice.

It's too soon to quit.

The Petrine Diaries:
Finish the Race

PETER'S SHTICK FOR A LONG TIME WAS THE SHOW-DOG entrance and the hangdog exit. Off the starting line the man was a fireball: zealous, undaunted, headlong, irrepressible. And then things would get hard. Obedience turned costly. Devotion got messy. Conviction became complicated.

And then his eyes scanned, desperate, for a runaway lane along the downward plunge of the road. His fingers traced, frantic, for an escape hatch embedded in the smooth floor. His hand groped, panicked, for an eject button somewhere on the tailspinning plane's cluttered panel.

It took Peter a long time to learn the principle of perseverance. It took many failures before he knew to stay the course. To put one foot in front of the other, day in, day out, day after day, week after week, month after month, year after year, no matter how difficult it got—that didn't come naturally to him. It took Peter a long time to understand that a brilliant beginning means nothing if you don't finish well.

There are so many incidents we could recall: his three denials, his floundering on the water, his complaining to Jesus about how bad the fishing was, you don't really want to head back out there, do you? There was his return to the boats and the nets even though Jesus had clearly, not once but twice, called him to a different line of work.

But it's the curious matter of pork I want to bring up.

The church's first major issue, a Gordian knot of theology and sociology and ecclesiology, was what to do with Gentile believers. The church that Jesus started had been nurtured in the cradle of Judaism. Its founder was Jewish, his first followers were Jewish, and though some of their practices were at sharp odds with current Pharisaical Judaism, the whole movement was deeply immersed in the rhythms and textures of Jewish life, in continuity with fundamental Jewish ways.

The idea that a good Christian would not be circumcised, not participate in the temple, not observe the dietary laws that had governed and made distinct this people for two thousand years or more—that idea at first didn't even occur to the apostles.

But then it did, and more suddenly than they had time to fully digest. It was always there, implicit in the Old Testament, increasingly explicit in Jesus's teaching: the good news was for all nations, not just one. When Jesus cleansed the temple, it was as much a protest against the nationalistic exclusivity that prevailed there as it was a frontal attack on the commercialization of religion. "My house will be called," Jesus declared, "a house of prayer for all nations" (Mark 11:17). It had become, not just a den of thieves, but a club for insiders.

No, the idea that Christ and the gospel were for the whole world had always been there, hidden in the soil of every covenant from Adam's to Abraham's, Moses' to David's, sprouting into broad daylight in the ministry of Jesus of Nazareth. The idea that the Spirit was to be poured on all people, already forecast by the prophets, was made plainly obvious on the day of Pentecost: even if all those who received the Spirit that day were Jewish, they were empowered for ministry to the very ends of the earth.

Only, the details were still fuzzy. As the gospel servants went out to the highways and byways to invite outsiders to the banquet, exactly what were the terms of the invitation? What was the dress code? What was on the menu? Whose standards of protocol were to be upheld? Whose rule book trumped whose?

It seemed obvious at first, beyond debate, that Gentile inclusion would be on Jewish terms. Of course the Gentiles would bend to Jewish laws and customs. Of course they would adopt the Jewish way of seeing things. Of course, they'd eat from our pantry, cooked the way we like.

Wouldn't they? The gospel was moving beyond the boundaries of Palestine rapidly, and sooner than anyone had time to fully weigh the issues, to ponder and deliberate them, the issues came looking for them, loud and urgent.

And then Peter fell into a trance. It was hunger-induced, perhaps heat-induced: he was praying at noon on his rooftop. Someone was in the kitchen preparing his lunch. The aroma from the cooking likely wafted up to him. Maybe it mingled with the smells of other neighborhood kitchens, other meals being prepared: bread baking, lamb roasting, yams boiling, spices bursting open beneath the fire's heat, releasing their hypnotic fragrance to the air. Something sweet and sticky for dessert. If he was hungry before, his hunger now became a kind of madness. His head grew light. His body seemed to split like a husk, shrivel to the ground; his spirit, wispy as a smoke trail, rose and danced.

He looked up, and out of heaven's brilliant vastness something descended. A sheet, held at four corners. At first Peter saw only the sheet's underbelly, a great billowing expanse, bulging and shadowy with whatever it held. But it touched earth and then he saw all that it contained: animals of every kind. The kind he ate, lambs and sheep and halibut and quail.

HIDDEN IN PLAIN SIGHT

And the kind he hated, pigs and prawns and conies.

And then a voice: "Get up, Peter. Kill and eat."

Peter protested vigorously, but the scene, the voice, repeated thrice. "Do not call anything impure that God has made clean," the voice declared, silencing all further protest.

Peter hardly had a moment to make sense of the whole thing when there was a knock at the door. Three men had come looking for him, sent by a centurion named Cornelius—three Gentiles sent by a Gentile, asking for Peter to return to the house of Cornelius with them. The Spirit told Peter directly, "Do not hesitate to go with them, for I have sent them." So Peter did. He entered the house of Cornelius and he "ate with them" (Acts 11).

And thus, with one noon-hour trance, two thousand years of Jewish dietary laws were overturned. To everyone's surprise, but very little dismay, it turned out that God intended the Gentile mission to be conducted largely on their terms.

But later, Peter flinched. The apostle Paul wrote to the Galatians about what happened:

When Peter came to Antioch, I opposed him to his face, because he was clearly in the wrong. Before certain men came from James, he used to eat with the Gentiles. But when they arrived, he began to draw back and separate himself from the Gentiles because he was afraid of those who belonged to the circumcision group. The other Jews joined him in his hypocrisy, so that by their hypocrisy even Barnabas was led astray.

When I saw that they were not acting in line with the truth of the gospel, I said to Peter in front of them all, "You are a Jew, yet you live like a Gentile and not like a Jew. How is it, then, that you force Gentiles to follow Jewish customs?" (Gal. 2:11–14)

For Paul, living "like a Gentile" was not a matter of expediency—finding the quickest, simplest way to reach the masses. It was a matter of theological essentials: "If righteousness could be gained through the law, Christ died for nothing!" (Gal. 2:21). Either Jesus's death on our behalf is wholly sufficient to secure salvation, or not. If it is, then what we eat or don't eat has no bearing whatsoever on the matter. Peter understood this—he was the first to get that revelation and to convince others of it. He was the first off the starting line.

How sad it would have been if he were the last to finish.

At least once, Peter needed Paul on his case, in his face, telling him he had been running a good race until someone cut in on him and kept him from obeying the truth (see Gal. 5:7). Telling him to get back in the race and run with perseverance. Telling him to stay the course.

The least Peter could do was pass the baton to us.

9

When I Grow Up:
Add to Your Faith . . . Godliness

IF YOU LOVE ME, YOU'LL LOVE ME AS I AM.

I use that line with my wife. She points out some minor flaw in me—I mean *minor*, minor as in petty, miniscule, incidental—and I retort, "If you love me, you'll love me as I am!" Love me with all my smells and noises, my quirks and whims, my warts and warps.

Well, it's true. The nature of deep love is its capacity to love what is unlovely, even unlovable. Deep love—what the Bible calls *agapē* love—transcends our inborn tendencies of attraction or revulsion. It subverts ingrained prejudice. It trumps our niggling irritations. It annuls our sticky and picky conditions.

Deep love loves simply because its nature is to love.

At just the right time, Paul says, *Christ died for us, while we were still sinners* (Rom. 5:8). When I was utterly unlovely and unlovable, God's love found me.

He loves me just as I am.

That's real love.

But that's only half of it.

Real love loves us, not just *as we are*, but *so that we can become what we are meant to be.* That, too, is its nature. It's a love that won't let us go. It is hardy and feisty and relentless. It loves at great cost. "For God so loved the world that he gave his one and only Son, that whoever believes in him shall not perish but have eternal life" (John 3:16).

Such love. It takes hold of us as we are, in our prodigal stench and squalor, but loves us until it makes us what we are to become, a son restored, cleansed head to toe, inside and out, dressed in royal robes, sated on fatted calf.

This chapter's virtue is not love. That comes later. Love is the crowning virtue in Peter's litany, but we won't get to it for a few pages yet.

This chapter's virtue is godliness. I mention love because godliness—*being Christlike in character*—is what God wants to love us into. It's the endpoint of divine love. When you have arrived at the fullness of godliness, the work of divine love is complete. It has accomplished what it set out to do.

This is a good place to repeat our key passage.

Simon Peter, a servant and apostle of Jesus Christ,

To those who through the righteousness of our God and Savior Jesus Christ have received a faith as precious as ours:

Grace and peace be yours in abundance through the knowledge of God and of Jesus our Lord.

His divine power has given us everything we need for life and godliness through our knowledge of him who called us by his own glory and goodness. Through these he has given us his very great and precious promises, so that through them you may participate in the divine nature and escape the corruption in the world caused by evil desires.

For this very reason, make every effort to add to your faith goodness; and to goodness, knowledge; and to knowledge, self-control; and to self-control, perseverance; and to perseverance, god-liness; and to godliness, brotherly kindness; and to brotherly kindness, love. For if you possess these qualities in increasing meas-ure, they will keep you from being ineffective and unproductive in your knowledge of our Lord Jesus Christ. But if anyone does not have them, he is nearsighted and blind, and has forgotten that he has been cleansed from his past sins. (2 Pet. 1:1–9)

All of which might be summarized in Peter's pithy command, *Be holy as God is holy* (1 Pet. 1:16), which he simply got from Leviticus (see Lev. 11:44–45).

BUT THERE ARE MOUNTAINOUS, TREACHEROUS OBSTACLES TO godliness. The work of becoming godly—holy and pure and Christlike—makes his work of conversion seem a simple matter. Conversion—where I was dead in sin but now am alive in Christ—is an astounding miracle, no question. But the miracle of godliness is, I think, greater yet—because with that, God not only makes me alive *in* Christ, he makes me to live *as* Christ.

Conversion makes spiritually dead people alive. God pulls that off in a blink.

Sanctification makes godless people godly. God typically uses a lifetime to accomplish that.

Our last chapter was perseverance. Perseverance—*hupomonē*—means to stand your ground. It's the refusal to turn tail and run just because things get dull or hard. You remain at your post. You do that, not out of stubbornness, pride, or stupidity, but because you're on the only road that leads home. There's nowhere else to go.

Perseverance comes where it does, in the middle of the list of virtues, because the virtue following it, godliness, will take all the time and endurance you've got. James says that we must let perseverance finish its work "so that you may be mature and complete, not lacking anything" (James 1:4). Perseverance has a work it sets out to do, and we must let it do its work. Its goal is to mature us. It is to complete us. It is to get us to the place where nothing is missing in our spiritual health.

It's to make us godly.

Let's take a step back and nail down a precise definition of *godliness*. In some ways, I've already given it: godliness is Christ-likeness. But let's tighten that up.

The Greek is *eusebeia*. It's the same word Peter uses in 2 Peter 1:3, where he says we already have everything we need for life and *godliness*. *Eusebeia*—sometimes translated *holiness*—means "good devotion" or "genuine devoutness." It describes the inward quality of a heart set completely on God, his kingdom, and his purposes. In short, *eusebeia* is *God-centeredness*.

Two New Testament passages lend special aid in helping us to grasp the substance of the word. The first is from Peter's first letter:

> But in your hearts set apart Christ as Lord. Always be prepared to give an answer to everyone who asks you to give the reason for the hope that you have. But do this with gentleness and respect, keeping a clear conscience, so that those who speak maliciously against your good behavior in Christ may be ashamed of their slander. (1 Pet. 3:15–16)

Godliness begins with a resolve of heart: *In your hearts, set apart Christ as Lord*. Before godliness shows up in our speech or actions or thinking, it takes hold in what we do with Jesus. Is Jesus at the table or still outside the door, knocking? Is Jesus telling you how it is, or are you telling Jesus what's what? *In your heart, set apart Jesus as Lord*. Everything follows from that.

But what does that mean? Simply, who Jesus is and what Jesus desires always—*always*—takes precedent. It takes precedent over our politics, our prejudices, our emotions, our upbringing, our opinions. All must step aside if in any way it stands in the way of Jesus and his kingdom.

In your hearts set apart Christ as Lord.

And then, right on the heels of that heart resolve, godliness requires a change of behavior. *Always be prepared to give a reason to everyone who asks*. Two things are clear here, one implicit, one explicit. The implicit thing is that godly people live in such a way that they arouse curiosity. They provoke questions. People start to wonder about them. They're different. Peculiar. They can't be accounted for by the usual theories, assumptions, and explanations.

That difference, that peculiarity, can be summed up in a word: *hope*. Godly people live in hope and offer hope. They bring hope into situations of fear and worry and despair and darkness and disappointment. Where others turn to complaining or panic or resignation or protest, the godly embrace hope. Peter is clear about where such hope springs from: ". . . your faith and *hope* are in God" (1 Pet. 1:21; emphasis mine). The hope of the godly is rooted in God, who can take the bleakest situations—crucifixion, death, the shattering of a dream—and turn it into the best thing imaginable. With a God like that, who wouldn't be hopeful?

That's what Peter makes implicit: godly people live lives so filled with hope they arouse wonder and provoke inquiry.

What he makes explicit is this: the godly are prepared to tell anyone who asks them about the reason for their hope. Godly people live in a readiness to seize opportunities that their peculiar living creates. When someone asks, "What is it about you, anyhow?" godly people don't get all tongue-tied and bashful. They don't say, "Well, I eat well, I exercise regularly, I try to get eight hours of sleep a night." No, they're ready to tell about the deep source of their hopefulness.

The third fact about the godly is that they seize those opportunities with grace. They show gentleness and respect to people. Godly people are not mouth-frothing, placard-waving, curse-spewing crusaders. They don't conceal or compromise who they are or what they believe—they do what they do with boldness and a clear conscience. But they're not arrogant or bullying about it, either. They don't shout at people or mock their beliefs or behaviour. They don't call down heaven's fire on every village that spurns them. They're not like Jonah, relishing the thought of doom for all who disagree with them.

They're more like Daniel, living "such good lives among the pagans that, though they accuse you of doing wrong, they may see your good deeds and glorify God on the day he visits us" (1 Pet. 2:12).

THE OTHER NEW TESTAMENT PASSAGE THAT HELPS US GRASP the meaning of godliness is from the pen of the apostle Paul.

> Beyond all question, the mystery of godliness is great:
> He appeared in a body,
> was vindicated by the Spirit,

> was seen by angels,
>
> was preached among the nations,
>
> was believed on in the world,
>
> was taken up in glory. (1 Tim. 3:16)

This passage follows Paul's instructions, justly famous, about the qualifications for elders and deacons. We rarely read this later verse in connection with those qualifications, but I think we should. 1 Timothy 3:16 is not only intimately related to the qualifications for leadership: it's essential to them. Godliness is not optional for any Christian, but for church leaders it is foundational. Before we look for anything else in a leader, we're to look for godliness. If that's absent, it matters little how otherwise gifted, wise, eloquent, or capable that person is. Godliness is the one ingredient that empowers and redeems all the others, and those who lead the church especially need to exhibit it.

Paul says godliness is a mystery. After all is said and done, there is no earthly explanation for it. The power for this kind of living is only available from above. It is a Spirit work, and there will always be an element of the inexplicable in it. It is born of the Spirit, and follows the Spirit and like the wind, "you cannot tell where it comes from or where it is going" (John 3:8). Once again, the godly are wonders, arousing curiosity.

But Paul's definition of godliness moves a step beyond Peter's. Peter says godliness begins when *in your heart you set apart Christ as Lord*. Paul adds that godliness also involves *setting your eyes upon Christ as Lord*. "You want the supreme example of godliness?" Paul, in effect, says. "Look to Jesus. He is the perfect embodiment of *eusebeia*."

He tells us six things about Jesus's godliness, and he implies that these six things are worthy of our imitation:

1. *Jesus appeared in a body.* The godly make God personal. They bring God close and render God's presence tangible. They incarnate heaven. When you stand among them, you sense God is near.

2. *Jesus was vindicated by the Spirit.* The godly entrust justice to God. They do not exhaust themselves trying to manage what others think about them. A primary enemy of godliness is our lust to be vindicated. When we feel misused, underappreciated, misunderstood, wrongfully accused, the temptation is to jump in and straighten everyone out. We squander vast reserves of energy in projects of self-vindication. But the godly know that in a fallen and broken world, being maligned or slandered is inevitable. They prefer a clear conscience to a spotless reputation, and trust the Spirit, in God's time, to vindicate them.

3. *Jesus was seen by angels.* The godly live with an awareness that the real drama takes place elsewhere, in a realm beyond the visible world. The main audience is cosmic, not earthly, angelic and demonic, not human. They believe that we are engaged in something much bigger than ourselves, bigger than earth can contain, bigger than mere humans can comprehend. They believe that their lives sometimes make little sense to the neighbors, or even to themselves, but that there is a throng of heavenly hosts watching with riveted, vested interest. The godly live in a way that makes angels cheer and demons quake.

4. *Jesus was preached among the nations.* The godly have global influence. Their identity and work casts a net far beyond the

narrow geography in which they move. They exert an influence far beyond the confines of their time and place.

5. *Jesus was believed on in the world.* The godly have impact beyond the church. Quite simply, they change the world they live in. They change the way people see, the things they believe, the values by which they live. Their influence translates into transformation.

6. *Jesus was taken up in glory.* The godly know their life has ultimate purpose and reward. They live in the here and now, but live with their eyes fixed on forever. They live in light of eternity. What motivates the godly is not earthly reward but the glory that will be revealed. Their treasure is in heaven.

That's godliness.

BUT THERE IS ONE ENORMOUS HURDLE.

Worldliness. The opposite of godliness is not devilry or demonism. That is the extreme opposite, but not the common, garden variety. Its opposite is worldliness. John describes worldliness this way: "For everything in the world—the cravings of sinful man, the lust of his eyes and the boasting of what he has and does—comes not from the Father but from the world" (1 John 2:16).

Worldliness is, in a word, selfishness. If godliness is God-centeredness, worldliness is self-centeredness. It's craving, lusting, boasting. It's me, me, me. It's getting what I want when I want it, and then ballyhooing about it. My own homespun definition of worldliness is this: *whatever makes sin look more attractive than God.*

It's whatever makes you think that defying or ignoring God will bring you more reward than obeying him.

Worldliness is not the same thing as earthiness. Earthiness is an admission of our limitations, frailties, needs, possibilities as humans made in the image of God. In fact, worldliness and earthiness are so different as almost to be opposites. At some level worldliness involves a denial of our humanness.

I mention this because the cure for worldliness and the path to godliness is in fact to become more human. It is to live in an awareness of your creatureliness and so your utter dependence on God. The worst thing you can do if you seek to be godly is to deny your creatureliness. You'll only end up faking it. Godliness is beautiful when it's authentic, and revolting when it's pretense.

So two things are needed.

One, look and look and look again to Jesus. Come to him, all you who are weary and heavy laden—he will give you rest for your soul, and more besides. As you abide in him, he promises, you will become like him.

Now all this is true and wonderful, but I myself have heard it so many times I'm almost immune to it. *Yeah, yeah*, is my unspoken response. *Fine. Good. Right. But what does it really mean?* Here's one way I've found to make this truth real: I actually juxtapose my own struggles—struggles in my actions, in my will, in my understanding, in my attitudes, in my emotions—with some story about Jesus. If I'm fretting over how others might see me, I return to the time the Pharisees asked Jesus to explain by what authority he said and did the things he did. Were I asked that question, my default would be to redouble my efforts to vouch for myself. I'd scramble to produce my credentials.

Jesus doesn't. He almost blithely, simply asks a question. *John the*

Baptist. *Was he from God or from man?* That stumps the boys, and so Jesus refuses to answer their other question.

I watch him closely. Jesus, I conclude, didn't really care how others saw him. He wouldn't testify on his own behalf. He was content to let God vindicate him. I sit with that until I can, at least in some small measure, imitate it.

I could go on, but I think you get the point. Because Jesus was tempted in every way that we are and yet was without sin, there is, in almost every particular of our trials and temptations, an example Jesus set so that we too might overcome. The apostle Paul, in that famous passage in Philippians where he calls all believers to have "the same attitude as that of Christ Jesus," begins by reminding us of the Jesus who abides with us:

> If you have any encouragement from being united with Christ, if any comfort from his love, if any fellowship with the Spirit, if any tenderness and compassion, then make my joy complete by being like-minded, having the same love. (Phil. 2:1–2)

Come near to God, and he will come near to you. Fix your eyes on Jesus, the author and perfecter of your faith. And then it's only a matter of time before you start taking on a resemblance.

So look and look and look again to Jesus.

And, two, practice and practice and practice the daily discipline of dying to yourself. This is worked out in the mundane more than the heroic. It is faithfulness in the small things before it can be carried off on the grand scale. It is the barb of sarcasm or the morsel of gossip or the retort of self-vindication that you *don't* speak. It is the flare-up of anger that you take to prayer rather than take out on your wife. It is the burning lust or haunting loneliness that you refuse to treat in the habitual way. It is the quiet prompting to give to another that you obey rather than squelch.

As a boy, I wanted to be a cowboy when I grew up, and if not that a fireman, or if not that a policeman. Something adventuresome, valorous, dangerous. Plus, with two of those vocations, you got to pack a gun, and with one wield an axe. It amazed me people were paid to do that.

I never became any of those, not even close. Some days—watching the cowboy in his sanctuary of earth and sky, or the fireman high in his steel-girded eyrie, wielding cannonades of water against a mayhem of flames, or the policeman looming over a car with a chastened driver inside, sullen and scrambling for his documents—some days I feel a pang of loss.

But only some days.

Because I'm setting my sights on something else, something higher, something that cowboys and firemen and cops and dentists and pastors and homemakers and students can all be when they grow up.

I want to be a saint.

The Petrine Diaries:
A Form of Godliness

THE APOSTLE PAUL WROTE HIS SO-CALLED PASTORAL EPISTLES—
1 and 2 Timothy, Titus—in his old age: a battle-scarred soldier, perhaps septuagenarian, not long for this world. I imagine his skin
yellowed and mottled like a pear left too long in the bowl, his
remaining scalp hair molted to gossamer wisps and silvery stubble.
His eyes smoky and glassy with near blindness. His hands trembling
from nerves tightening and loosing under their own dark counsel.

He'd earned a right to speak. Where in earlier letters we sense in
him at times a testiness—an upstart staking his territory, flaunting
his credentials, working out pecking orders—in the Pastoral Epistles
he's mannered and serene, an elder statesman calmly distilling his
hard-won wisdom for the next generation. Like Jacob, "By faith,
[he], when he was dying, blessed each of Joseph's sons, and wor-
shipped as he leaned on the top of his staff" (Heb. 11:21). That's
Paul. He's going to finish well, blessing those who come behind
him, worshipping to his last breath.

In the midst of all his sage counsel, then, his sudden vigor in
2 Timothy 3, his outburst of doomsaying and rancor, is startling:

> But mark this: There will be terrible times in the last days. People
> will be lovers of themselves, lovers of money, boastful, proud, abu-
> sive, disobedient to their parents, ungrateful, unholy, without love,

unforgiving, slanderous, without self-control, brutal, not lovers of the good, treacherous, rash, conceited, lovers of pleasure rather than lovers of God—having a form of godliness but denying its power. Have nothing to do with them. (2 Tim. 3:1–5)

But mark this. You can almost see him rise from his chair, index finger thrust upward, face pulled taut, voice striking each word with the hardness of metal. Some things still get his blood boiling. He must have seen a lot of these types, slick and shallow, cloaking daggers beneath flattery. He must have seen the deep and lasting damage they do to his beloved church. "When a lion or a bear came and carried off a sheep from the flock, I went after it" (1 Sam. 17:34–35). The warrior's still in Paul, awakened, always, by any threat to the gospel and the bride.

And what provokes him most is a form of godliness that denies its power. "Always learning," he further describes such people, "but never able to acknowledge the truth" (2 Tim. 3:7). Always attending seminars, reading books, crusading for or against the latest fad, always confessing others' sins and fixing others' problems. They know so much, except what would set them free.

He'd seen a lot of these kinds of people (some he even names). Every pastor has.

It's the man who can quote more scriptures than the minister, but is raping his daughter. It's the woman who is praising the Lord, praising him every time she picks up the phone to spread rumors and dissension. It's the businessman who loudly thanks God for his success, but mistreats and underpays his workers. It's the teen who is one thing at church and another everywhere else. It's the couple who maintains an impeccable semblance of piety—fish plaques on their cars, children in the Christian school, speech soaked in Bible verses—but who behind closed doors tears each other apart. It's the man on the church council who denounces gays and liberals and tattoos and poodles, but who goes home and, when his wife is asleep, pulls up Internet sites that would make Caligula blush.

It's people for whom Jesus is always on their lips and far from their hearts. It's people whose form of godliness is a just a cheap disguise for deep-rooted habits of godlessness.

Every pastor knows them.

Including Pastor Pete. Peter, I mean. We usually don't think of Peter as a pastor, but that's how I read Jesus's charge to him on the lakeshore a few days after the Resurrection. *Peter*, he asks, *do you love me?* Three times he asks, three times Peter says *yes*.

Then feed my sheep. Care for my lambs. Make sure the ones I love, I died for, I am chief shepherd over—make sure they get good things to eat, and can enjoy it in safe pasture. If a bear or a lion come and carry one of my flock away, go after it (see 1 Sam. 17:34–35).

Which is ironic, Peter being a pastor, a shepherd, entrusted with the care of sheep and lambs, instructed in their feeding regimen, their grazing habits. It's ironic because there was a time, not long before Peter's lakeshore ordination, when he might easily have fit the description of one who had a form of godliness but denied its power. He was not, not ever, all those terrible things Paul rails against. Sometimes he could be "boastful, proud," but little else in Paul's damning portrait looks anything like him.

Except, it's that word *denial* we can't avoid. *But denying its power . . . never able to acknowledge the truth.* Peter will, as long as earth remains, bear the stigma of what happened that night, and what didn't happen. He denied the power, and *the Power*. He was unable to acknowledge the truth, and *the Truth*. He denied Christ three times, but in those denials he denied much else besides:

God's sovereign goodness, God's redemptive purposes, even in suffering, God's upside-down kingdom.

He knew it right away, is the good thing. But knowing didn't help. It thrust him into remorse and made him bitter with sorrow. And the story might have ended there, were it not for Jesus's severe mercy and restoring grace.

And so Simon Peter became the chief apostle, wielding enormous influence. If Simon says we now eat prawns and pork, so be it. If Simon says the Samaritans are now included in the Spirit's work, it is so. What Simon says, others do.

Jesus took a man who had abandoned his post like a hireling and turned him into a shepherd after his own heart, and filled him full with heaven's authority.

With power like that, it's sheer craziness to deny it.

10

Where's Your Brother?
Add to Your Faith . . .
Brotherly Kindness

GOD LOVES QUESTIONS. OF ALL HIS ATTRIBUTES, PERHAPS HIS curiosity is the one we notice least. But he possesses a relentless inquisitiveness. He has, from the garden right up to your prayer time this morning, peppered us with inquiry. In the sweeping wideness and piercing deepness of his knowing, he must possess already, in utmost fullness, answers to what he asks.

He asks anyhow.

"Where is your brother?"

It's this question, God's fourth by my count, that of late gives me pause. He asks it of Cain, Adam and Eve's firstborn.

Cain has a younger brother, Abel. Life seems to work for Abel in a way it doesn't for Cain. God, it seems, lavished Abel with tenfold talents, and stinted Cain with one. Abel's the golden boy, the favorite. He walks into windfalls, sidesteps pitfalls. Good fortune downright chases the boy. What he touches flourishes.

What Cain touches withers, is what it feels like to him.

So Cain despises Abel. It began in a burning wildness of envy. It started—of all places—in church, when Abel's worship won God's heart and Cain's worship didn't. Cain's initial flare-up of anger cooled and narrowed and hardened, until it became an icy sliver of pure hate. His envy turned to rancor, his rancor to vengefulness, and vengefulness then bloomed into a plan.

Cain is, we sense, a big man, capable of great damage with just his hands, rending and crushing. He's brooded awhile on this personal affront. He can't make up his mind whether God or his brother is the main culprit. He decides it's both.

So one day, cloaking dark intent behind kind gesture, in a taut masquerade of brotherliness, he asks Abel to join him in the fields. Abel, I think, is delighted. He is, we sense, a touch naive. Overly trusting. No doubt he's sensed Cain's contempt for him, heard it in the hardness of his voice, read it in the stiffness of his posture, seen it in the restrained violence of his motions. But this sign of a truce thrills him.

So he goes with him, out to the field. And there, on the very ground Cain plows and sows and reaps, Cain sets upon brother Abel. He hits him and hits him and hits him until his red blood stains the earth black. He hits him until Abel stops begging Cain to stop, stops encircling his own head with his thin arms, stops heaving, stops moaning, stops twitching, stops moving altogether, stops making any sound at all.

And then, strangely, God shows up. An hour late, it would seem.

"Where is your brother?" God asks Cain.

"I don't know," Cain says, aloof, defiant. "Am I my brother's keeper?"

Cain's story is a twisted variation on the parable of the talents. In Jesus's story, the man with one talent buries it, and returns it intact when the master comes asking. In this story, the man with the single talent buries the man with the ten, and pretends to know nothing of his whereabouts when the master comes asking.

ON THE MATTER OF BROTHERHOOD, THE BIBLE IS NOTHING IF NOT realistic. It treats the topic with unflinching honesty. Brothers struggle with each other. Jacob and Esau. Joseph and his brothers. David, and his. Jesus, and his. These are stories of betrayal and deceit, jealousy and rivalry, rejection and revenge.

And yet there are also stories of brothers—indeed, many of the same stories—that are about sacrifice and courage, mercy and reconciliation, love and welcome.

Where is your brother? That question, asked in a lonely field long ago, still haunts us. Maybe, in our day of renewed tribalism and factionalism, when people divide over the slimmest of causes, the question is more poignant than ever.

Where is my brother? Who is my brother? Am I my brother's keeper?

Peter says this: "For this very reason, make every effort to add to your faith . . . brotherly kindness" (2 Pet. 1:5–7).

BROTHERLY KINDNESS IS PETER'S SECOND-TO-LAST VIRTUE. The word he uses is *philadelphia*, though there are other words he might have used. Two words, in fact, would have been more natural choices in some ways: the ever-popular *chrēstotēs,* and the equally available *philanthropia*. The first describes goodwill that gives rise to kind deeds. The second, love toward mankind that expresses itself in acts of selfless generosity.

Both are great words for kindness.

But Peter chose *philadelphia*. *Brotherly love*. He actually—we'll see this in a moment—has to change its meaning somewhat to shoe-horn it into his scheme of virtues. And he does this, I think, because he knew that something more, something deeper than mere kindness is called for in the Christian life. *Chrēstotēs, philanthropia*—those can be done at a distance, with a certain detachment. Philanthropy is usually anonymous: a rich man in his mansion writes a check, and little orphans in a shantytown get new clothes.

It doesn't have to be personal.

But *philadelphia* does. Brotherly kindness is me caring for you and you for me, up close, face-to-face, hands-on. Unless I am willing to bear with you and you with me—putting up with each other, in all our oddness and weirdness and prickliness—then all we have is philanthropy. That's a nice enough thing, but it is a sad substitute for *philadelphia*. *Philadelphia* asks, *Who is my brother? Where is my brother?* And it insists, *I am my brother's keeper. Philadelphia* gets involved. It comes near. As James—the brother to Jesus himself—puts it, "Suppose a brother or sister is without clothes and daily food. If one of you says to him, 'Go, I wish you well; keep warm and well fed,' but does nothing about his physical needs, what good is it?" (James 2:15–16).

Unless there's *philadelphia*—a brotherly kindness that gets personal and practical—what good is it?

There's another reason, I think, Peter chose this word. A more accurate rendering of *philadelphia* is brotherly *love*. That's how the word *phila* and *phileō* and its derivatives get translated everywhere except here, in 2 Peter. Here, English translators render *phila* as *kindness*, probably because they don't want to confuse us. The seventh and last virtue in Peter's list is love. So to avoid the appearance of redundancy, they translate this virtue as *kindness*, not *love*.

Which is too bad. Because I believe Peter is making a deliberate point. When we get to our last virtue, we'll see that the word Peter uses for love is *agapē*, that justly famous word. Sometimes preachers and commentators make a sharp distinction between *phileo* and *agapē*. They argue that *phileo* is a sort of hesitant love, waiting for the other to make the first move, dependent on a the response of the other, whereas *agapē* is a fierce, pure, lofty form of love, given regardless of how it's received. We'll talk more about this in the next chapter.

But that distinction is often overdone. Peter is not particularly concerned with a lot of hair-splitting over semantics. He's not ranking one love above the other. The point I think Peter wants to make is that we need both forms of love, *phileo* and *agapē*. We don't prefer one over the other. We make every effort to acquire both and grow in them. The Christian life is incomplete otherwise.

And this is why: *Philadelphia* is to love *what* God loves. *Agapē* is to love *as* God loves. Or, put another way, the first is to love *whom* God does, the other to love *in the way* God does.

So who does God love? Find that out and that's your brother, and you're his keeper.

THE WORD *PHILADELPHIA* IS COMMON OUTSIDE THE BIBLE, but used in ways significantly different from the way the Bible uses it. The Greeks, without exception, denoted by it biological love. It described the special bond between blood brothers—and blood brothers meant male siblings *from the same father*, not necessarily the same mother. Among pagans, *philadelphia* was another way of saying blood is thicker than water. It was shorthand for "family sticks together, always."

The New Testament writers took this word and flipped it inside out. It still means, in the hands of John and Paul and Peter, love between brothers. Only, they radically alter the definition of brother and sister. A brother or sister no longer means blood relative. It means, not those who share bloodline, but those who have been washed in the blood of Christ.

This is revolutionary. The New Testament hijacks a term that was meant to be exclusive, to circumscribe our singular obligations to family, and almost inverts it. The exclusivity of the term becomes, in their hands, inclusive. The circle of our affections and obligations hugely expands. *Where is my brother?* It's you. We are as bound to each other as if we had the same father.

Which of course we do. That is the deeper and more radical shift Peter and the others make. They don't so much redefine brotherhood and sisterhood: they redefine fatherhood. They retain the root meaning of *philadelphia*: love between those from the same father. So the real question is not, *Where is my brother?* It is, *Where and who is my father?*

Our Father, who art in heaven . . .

It's crucial we grasp this. If my Father is God, and your Father is God, then we are children of the same Father. And that makes us kin.

And if I love the Father, I will also love what the Father loves, and more than anything that's his children. Christopher. Linda. Sue. Bill. My brothers and sisters. As an expression of my love for the Father, I must love them also. I must love whom the Father loves.

Not all of them are lovable. They're curmudgeonly, some of them, and others boring, and a few obnoxious. This one has a grating laugh, and that one an ingratiating manner. Some I don't want to talk with, and some I want to talk about behind their backs. Some I want to avoid. Some I want to put in their place.

But they're brothers and sisters, children of the same Father, and as John says, annoyingly, *Anyone who says he loves God but doesn't love his brother is a liar* (1 John 4:20).

To love God is to love what God loves. *Philadelphia* is *refracted* affection. Refraction is the process where an object changes, in shape, in size, in appearance, by passing through a medium. A prism refracts a thread of white light into a fantail of color. Water refracts a straight stick so that it crooks and swells in appearance.

Philadelphia is refracted affection. God refracts the thin white thread of our love for him into a thick vibrant band of love for others. I am incapable of loving someone else unconditionally. But if I love God first and most, I can love what he loves, and even, through a long obedience in the same direction, as he loves.

BROTHERLY KINDNESS HAS FOUR EXPRESSIONS.

The first is equality. With brothers, none has status above the other. It doesn't matter what role you play within the family, as brothers and sisters there are no "favorites." James makes this explicit: *My brothers,* he says, *as believers in our glorious Lord Jesus—as children of the same father—don't show favoritism* (James 2:1). Don't prefer one over the other. Don't give access or privilege to someone at the expense of someone else. James illustrates what he means with an example of how we are prone to pamper and flatter the rich and snub and abuse the poor. *That's favoritism,* James says, *and it's evil.* Jesus puts the matter this way: "You are not to be called 'Rabbi,' for you have only one Master *and you are all brothers*" (Matt. 23:8; emphasis mine). Don't bestow exalted status on anyone. You are all equals here.

The second expression of brotherhood is unity. Jesus prays for all believers in John 17 that this would be the one sign above all that

HIDDEN IN PLAIN SIGHT

we are *all children of the same father.* Six times in that prayer Jesus calls God *Father,* and with each repetition he intensifies the implication of unity: just as Jesus and the Father are one, so those whom the Father has adopted as his children should be one. "My prayer," Jesus says, "is . . . that all of them may be one, Father, just as you are in me and I am in you" (John 17:20–21). Christian unity at its deepest and yet simplest is this: Jesus Christ indwells you and he indwells me. We have been joined to the Father through the work of Jesus and the presence of the Spirit. So whatever makes us different could not possibly be greater than what makes us alike. Whatever divides us cannot possibly be stronger than what brings us together. If Jesus Christ is with you, and Jesus Christ is with me, then what we have in common exceeds everything we don't.

The third expression of brotherhood is closeness. The imagery of brotherhood implies a warmth of feeling toward one another, a desire for intimacy with each other, a bond that transcends mere friendship. "My brothers," Paul says to the Philippians, "you whom I love and long for, my joy and crown" (Phil. 4:1). He openly and without embarrassment expresses his heart. He might feel awkward doing that, except these are his brothers and sisters, all children of the same father. As people grow older, they typically have a stronger yearning to be among family. The brother or sister that maybe we were estranged from growing up, or just never really connected with—we begin to miss deeply. We ache for closeness. Many are the stories of family members who only really learn to love late in life.

So it should be in the family of God. One measure of whether you are really growing in your faith is that you are experiencing an increased desire to get close to other Christians. If the love of the Father is really alive in you, *philadelphia* will be a natural symptom. In fact, if you are feeling more distant from the people of God, that is a sure signal that something in your love of the Father has gone askew. My advice is, quick as you can, come back into a deep abiding in the Father's love.

The fourth expression is servanthood. Paul makes this clear in Romans 12, which is all about each of us serving the other for the sake of the body and the glory of God. In verse 10, Paul says, "Be devoted to one another in brotherly love [*philadelphia*]. Honor one another above yourselves."

Simply, love serves. Love honors. Love is practical devotion that seeks the good of the other.

Equality. Unity. Closeness. Servanthood.

This is serious stuff. "We know that we have passed from death to life," John says, "because we love our brothers. Anyone who does not love remains in death." And then he puts it even more starkly: "Anyone who hates his brother is a murderer, and you know that no murderer has eternal life in him" (1 John 3:14–15).

Philadelphia, the quality of our brotherly kindness, divides those who have life from those who, Cain-like, only take it.

A NUMBER OF YEARS AGO, I WAS STRUGGLING WITH MY ATTITUDE toward another Christian. I fed my resentment and bitterness to the point where at times I hated this person. One day, when I was thinking nasty thoughts about him, I heard my son come in the basement, slam the door, go to his room, and start crying. I went to him and asked what was wrong. He'd been playing goalie in a game of road hockey with some school friends, he told me, and he'd let in a rash of goals. His teammates started taunting him, mocking him, telling him he was useless, telling him to go home. They'd stand a better chance with an empty net than with him in it.

I was furious. I was enraged. I started putting on my shoes to march down the road, call those boys to account, give them all a hard drubbing with my tongue.

"Mark," God said, "where are you going?"

"To straighten this matter out, Lord. No one treats my son that way."

"You have a father's heart," God said.

"Yes!"

"You hate it when someone hurts one of your children."

"Yes!"

"I hate that, too," God said.

And I understood in the most visceral way, and I think for the very first time, that I could not claim to love God and hate my brother. If I love God, I'll love what he loves. I'll love his children, all of them.

Or else, break his heart.

The Petrine Diaries:
O Brother, Where Art Thou?

BROTHERHOOD WAS TRICKY FOR PETER. HE HAD A BROTHER, Andrew, one of Jesus's first disciples. Andrew met and followed Jesus before Peter did. In fact, Andrew introduced Peter to Jesus. Then Peter stepped forward, and Andrew stepped back, and Andrew disappeared beneath Peter's tall, wide shadow, hardly ever to be seen again.

Andrew leaves nary a stain in the Gospel accounts. He gets named in the registry of apostles. He hovers in the background. He never speaks, except in a generic way, as part of a group. He usually is mentioned with this tag: "the brother of Peter." How enraging that must have been. *I was here first. If not for me, Peter would never have gotten here!*

Brother of. People hate to be introduced merely as the "husband of, the sister of, the nephew of . . ." That feels like the ultimate eclipsing of our uniqueness. We are subsumed by another, only existing by virtue of some thin claim of association we have to them. Andrew is Peter's appendage, Peter's addendum, Peter's footnote. He has virtually no identity outside his relationship to the chief apostle. It didn't matter that he was there first. Now, he's just the *brother of.*

Peter was also in the thick with two other brother-apostles, James and John. He saw their shenanigans, their conspiratorial antics and wily schemes, the way they ganged up, tag-team-like, to maneuver their way to the front of the line, the way they plotted, at the urging of their mother, like two Jacobs with scheming Rebekah, coups and identity thefts. He saw their violent tempers, and how they were just as prone as he was to instruct Jesus on the best course of action to take, such as firebombing a few Samaritan villages to punish their inhospitableness (see Luke 9:54).

Peter knew brotherhood's unique intricacies.

Brotherly kindness is not as natural as it first appears. Brothers, for one, aren't always kind, not to each other, not to others. Being siblings is just as likely to generate rivalry and envy, suspicion and disdain, as it is goodwill and oneness. A woman once confessed to me that her intense dislike for a woman in our church had nothing at all to do with the woman. "She reminds me of my sister," she said. "My sister always did everything better than me. *Oh, you're so pretty*, everyone always told her. *You're so thin, so talented, so funny.* They never said that to me. So I hated her, and I hate anyone who reminds me of her."

"Tell my brother to divide the inheritance with me," is how one man interrupts Jesus and prompts from him a famous parable (see Luke 12:13ff). Jesus's initial retort: "Man, who appointed me judge or arbiter between you?" Jesus is in the reconciling business, not the dividing one. He wants to join things together, not break them asunder.

It turns out, we need as much grace—and sometimes, more—to love our brother as we do to love our neighbor, or a stranger, or even our enemy. Sometimes our brother is our enemy: I can think of many people I know who have not spoken to a sibling in more than ten years, in some cases in many decades.

It's John—John, of all people, angry, hawkish, rival-bound John—

who tells us that we can't love God if we don't also love our brother (see 1 John 4:20). And all the writers of the New Testament agree that in Christ, the terms of brotherhood and sisterhood are multiplied exponentially: now, my brother and sister are not those with whom I shared a womb, not just those whose bloodline I have in common, but those who, like me, have been washed in the blood of the Lamb. Those with whom I'm heaven-bound and Christ-sworn. Jesus himself said, *Whoever does God's will is my brother and sister and mother* (see Mark 3:33–35).

Peter, calling us to grow in brotherly kindness, is saying more than at first meets the eye. He is asking us, not just to settle for natural affection—even at the best of times, that is a meagre thing—but to rise to Christlike altruism. "Both the one who makes men holy and those who are made holy are of the same family. So Jesus is not ashamed to call them brothers" (Heb. 2:11).

Where is your brother? He might be closer than you think. Love the one whom Jesus loves, the one he's chosen, the one in whom he is at work to make holy. Cast out your spirit of sibling rivalry by the Spirit that has made you a son or daughter of *Abba*, the Father God. Do not miss the grace of God and so become like Cain, cursed and estranged, exiled from the very place he sought, by killing his brother to have all to himself.

Tradition has it that Peter presides over the entrance to heaven, enthroned before the kingdom's pearly gates. Maybe it's so. Who knows?

But I wouldn't be surprised, were it true, that some days he lets Andrew sit there.

11

The Perfection of Heaven:
Add to Your Faith . . . Love

G. K. CHESTERTON, THAT OVERSIZED GNOME, THAT MIRTHFUL gadfly, was one of the first people to notice the grown-up value of fairy tales. Fairy tales more than childish diversions, more than juvenile capers: at their best, they show us how to live wisely, with shrewdness and innocence, neither being wolfish nor duped by wolfish wiles, tricking witches but not by witchy guile, plundering giants and dragons without succumbing to dragonish greed, giant like malice. Outwitting the devil but never by devilry. These stories distill vice. They magnify virtue. They extol courage and scorn cowardice, but in a visceral way, so that our blood boils or chills at the telling. We take these stories in with our mothers' milk, and they help make our souls straight and sturdy just like milk does for our bones. They whisper their wisdom to us lifelong.

Chesterton's most treasured fable was *Beauty and the Beast*. The chief lesson of that story, he said, was this: "Unlovely things must be deeply loved before they become lovable."

An earlier story—only this one not a fairy tale—taught us exactly that.

While we were yet sinners, Christ died for us.

Unlovely things must be deeply loved before they become lovable.

WE ARRIVE AT PETER'S FINAL AND CROWNING VIRTUE.

Love.

If we'd received even only a rough apprenticeship in the Christian life, and no more than a glancing exposure to the Word of God, we'd have guessed this anyhow: love drenches the pages of Scripture. Paul says that if we possess every other spiritual power but lack love, all's worthless. Peter says that, above everything, we must love each other deeply. John says that love is the sign that we're born of God, that we belong to God, that we've crossed from death into life—indeed, he says, God *is* love. Jesus says that our love for others is the clearest evidence that we're truly his disciples.

Love heralds and completes and fulfills what it means to live in God and for God. There is legend about the apostle John—John, that old firebrand, the Son of Thunder with a mean streak a mile wide, whom Christ loved until he became the Apostle of Love. The hawk who, by the alchemy of Jesus's affection, turned dove. The legend is that John lay dying, wizened and rickety, and his brokenhearted community gathered round him and begged him to impart one last word. He mustered his final breath and said, "Love one another."

He fell silent.

"Is there more?" they asked.

"That is enough," he said.[1]

THE WORD PETER USES FOR LOVE IS FAMOUS BECAUSE HE AND other New Testament writers made it so: *Agapē. Agapē* is often described as unconditional love, which is accurate. Conditional love, love predicated on desire and expectation, takes an *if . . . then* form. *If* you are good, if you please me, if you return love to me, if you are beautiful and you remain so . . . *then* I will love you.

With conditional love, decision follows emotion: I *feel* love; therefore, I *will* love.

Agapē works the opposite way. With *agapē, emotion follows decision. Agapē* is not emotionless—no love is—but its emotion is the fruit of decision: I *will* love; therefore, I *feel* love.

But actually, *agapē* is even more hardy and stubborn than that: it wills love even in the face of fierce resistance. *Agapē* chooses to love, not just *before* there is emotion, but sometimes *in spite of* other emotions that otherwise come naturally. It loves in the face of betrayal, in the face of rejection, in the face of evasion, in the face of rank badness. It wills love even when circumstances trigger instincts of anger or hurt, withdrawal or revenge. *Agapē* builds its house, often, in the ruins.

Agapē, then, is not a *because of* love; it's an *in spite of* love. It's love of the great nevertheless. It exists free of conditions, fueled by something within itself rather than evoked by something outside itself.

But here is even a simpler and, I think, more precise way to understand *agapē*: it is *unprovoked love*. I have never heard it described that way, but I think that describes it best. We use the term "unprovoked" in relation to anger or violence or attack. We read in the paper or hear on the news about some incident of "unprovoked aggression," or some such. There was John Doe, minding his business at the bus stop, and along came a gang of thugs to beat and rob him in an "unprovoked attack."

We never use that word in connection with love. You never read, "There was John Doe, minding his business at the bus stop, and along came a group of altruists and philanthropists who blessed him in an act of 'unprovoked love.'" Yet isn't that exactly what happened in the story of the Good Samaritan? An act of unprovoked love reversed an act of unprovoked violence. Love covered over a multitude of sins.

Agapē is unprovoked love: it seeks those who never saw it coming, who never *had* it coming, who never sought it out. It shows up unannounced, unexpected, undeserved. It doesn't rise up to our beauty. It doesn't ride in on our popularity. It doesn't depend upon our worthiness. It doesn't hang in due to our good manners. It doesn't back off because of our clumsiness, or homeliness, or churlishness. It pursues us, and even when unrequited, pursues us still. It finds us in a ditch and, at personal cost and personal risk, without reward, lifts us up and mends our wounds, and finds us shelter.

All unprovoked.

We attribute acts of unprovoked anger or violence to some moral flaw in the perpetrator. We ascribe it to something amiss inside the person. They're broken in some way, twisted, messed up. Their mothers made them wear funny pants, and now they're wreaking havoc for it, taking vengeance on an innocent passerby. Their rage is without due cause. They're angry for no reason. It's just the way they are.

Unprovoked love works on the same principle but in the opposite direction. When we witness it, we have to attribute it to something inside the perpetrator, some moral perfection, something complete, something solid, some deep and astonishing good that's there. It is affection without due cause. It's love for no reason, love beyond reason. It's just the way they are.

And yet I don't want to create the impression that *agapē* just *happens* to anyone. You can't fall into or out of *agapē*. It is a choice. *Agapē* lovers don't sing with Elvis: "I can't help falling in love with you."

They *can* help it. That's just the point: they choose it.

And they do because this is how God is. You've heard of Latin lovers. God's an *agapē* lover. His love is unprovoked. It's chosen. And God wants us to be *agapē* lovers, too. As I said last chapter, *philadelphia,* brotherly love, is loving *what* God loves. *Agapē,* unprovoked love, is loving *as* God loves.

Later, we'll explore how to become more of an *agapē* lover. But first, let's look at where *agapē* shines brightest and is needed most. It's among, especially, three kinds of people: The *least of these,* the *most of these,* and the *worst of these.*

Losers.

Winners.

Enemies.

THE *LEAST OF THESE* IS THAT PERSON YOU'RE MOST LIKELY *NOT* to notice. In our busyness, our competitiveness, our selfishness, it's easy to ignore and rush past *least of these* people. *Agapē,* once chosen, begins to subvert our haste and indifference. It overturns our natural inclinations of disdain, disgust, apathy. It strips our sense of superiority. It breaks our attachment to comfort and security. *Agapē* pushes us beyond ourselves.

And one of its first signs is that we start to care for those whom, without love, we're tempted to trample or sidestep. Jesus calls these people the *least of these*: the beggar, the prisoner, the refugee, the homeless man. He says the primary litmus test of whether or not we are truly his disciples is our capacity to notice such people and to commit acts of unprovoked love toward them: glasses of cold water to thirsty ragamuffins, clothes to bedraggled refugees, hot meals for disheveled panhandlers.

Recently, I've started reading the story of Christ clearing the temple through different eyes. Jesus braids cords into a whip and, white-hot with anger, chases money changers and merchants from the temple courts. For years I read this, as I think most of us have, as Jesus's condemnation on religious commercialism, where worship becomes one more transaction, one more form of trafficking and deal making. I still read it that way, but I've also started to notice something else, and maybe more primary, in the story: Jesus's anger over the way all that commercial activity creates barriers to the very people who need the temple's ministrations the most. Jesus was denouncing, not just profiteering in the name of God, but also the entrenchment of an economic system that excluded the least of these.

How do I derive that? It has to do with what Jesus says when he clears the temple, and what Jesus does afterward. What he says is that buying and selling in the temple has corrupted its God-ordained purpose, has made a "den of robbers" out what is to be "a house of prayer *for all nations*" (Mark 11:17; emphasis mine).

For all nations. Prayer is the casualty of greed, but so is a spirit of welcome. The temple rulers have embraced practices that homogenize the place, that cater to and welcome in one kind of people only: our kind.

And then there's what Jesus does afterward. According to Matthew's Gospel, he invites into the freshly cleansed temple the sick: "The blind and lame came to him . . . and he healed them" (Matt. 21:14). He cleaned things up to host the broken.

A house of prayer for all nations. A house of healing for all people. The very people who needed access to the temple most were, prior to Christ's cleansing, kept farthest away.

But God cares about the least of these—the outcast, the marginalized, the forgotten, the despised—and he'll overturn tables, and structures, and systems, and chase out with a whip those who build and manage them, to make room for the least of these.

It's simply the way *agapē* works.

In Brooklyn, New York, there is a school for children with learning disabilities called Chush. A few years ago, a father of one of the students, Shaya, spoke at a fundraising dinner for the school. He began mildly enough, thanking this person and that person. Then he startled everyone with an anguished question: "Where is the perfection in my son, Shaya? Everything done in heaven is done with perfection. But my child cannot understand things as other children do. . . . Where is the perfection in that?"

The guests sat silent.

"I believe," the man continued, "that when heaven brings a child like this into the world, the perfection it seeks is in the way people react to this child."

He then told a story. One day he and Shaya were watching some boys play softball. Shaya wanted to play, and the father went over and spoke with the pitcher of one of the teams. The boy was at first unsure. Then he shrugged and said, "Whatever. We're in the eighth inning and behind by six runs. We've got nothing to lose. Sure. He can play short center field. We'll let him bat in the ninth."

Shaya was ecstatic. He shambled out to his position and stood there.

But by the bottom of the ninth, his team had fallen behind by two points and had the bases loaded. They needed a home run to make it work—only, Shaya was scheduled to bat. The boys conferred, and to the father's amazement they handed the bat to Shaya. He stood over the base, clutching the bat askew, too tight. The pitcher from the opposing team then did a remarkable thing: he took several steps closer, and lobbed an easy ball right over the plate. Shaya swung wildly and missed widely. One of his teammates came up and wrapped his arms around Shaya from behind, and together they held the bat. The pitcher lobbed another easy ball, and Shaya and his teammate bunted it. It rolled right to the pitcher. All the players shouted for Shaya to run to first. He shuffled along. The pitcher could have had an easy out, but he threw the ball wide and far to left field. Shaya made first base. The players yelled for him to take second. Again, the catcher in left field threw wide and far, and Shaya made second. On it went, the other players all making home plate, Shaya loping along and everyone from both sides screaming themselves hoarse for him to run all the way. He touched home plate, and the ball came singing in behind him. The boys cheered madly. They mounted Shaya on their shoulders and paraded him as a hero.

"That day," the father said, "Those eighteen boys reached their level of heaven's perfection."[2]

That day they chose to commit an act of unprovoked love.

BUT COMPARATIVELY SPEAKING, IT'S EASY TO LOVE THE LEAST of these. The least of these is Shaya. Shaya is sweet. Shaya is innocent. Shaya does no wrong. Shaya means no harm.

Agapē calls us further still—to love *the most of these*. The *most of these* is that person who does what you do, only better. Maybe much better. It's the person you, as well as everyone else, are *most likely* to notice, and resent. Your rival. The one who threatens to eclipse you.

It's your prettier sister. It's your more athletic brother. It's the worship team singer who everyone raves about when you're standing right there, and you sing too. It's the preacher they fawn over, the artist they gush about, the dancer they adore. It's the man with ten talents to the man with only one. It's David to Saul. It's Abel to Cain. It's Joseph to his brothers. It's Mozart to Salieri.

Agapē pushes us beyond ourselves to help us overcome our inborn jealousies or resentments toward such people. It trumps our feeling of inferiority and insecurity.

I feel no threat from heart surgeons, pottery makers, French chefs, pool sharks. Tap dancers bother me not a whit.

It's writers who make me nervous.

The most of these is that person who excels in the area you want to excel, and maybe do. They just excel more. Their presence makes you nearly invisible. *Agapē* allows us to cheer that person when our inclination is to jeer them, or gossip about them, or find the worm in their apple. It frees us to be our biggest rival's biggest fan. Indeed, if we show *agapē* here, we actually go beyond God. God doesn't need to practice *agapē* love toward *the most of these* because nobody is God's superior. Nobody does it better. No one is a more gifted creator, a more accomplished singer, a more talented artist, a more compassionate caregiver. God's got us beat, hands down.

But someone somewhere is better than you. And when that person is close by, it takes more than human affection to really embrace him. It calls for *agapē*.

One of the most remarkable stories in the Bible about this is the account of the friendship between David and Jonathan, the son of King Saul. King Saul was the first person who, without divine aid, saw David's enormous giftedness. What David's father and brothers had missed, what the prophet Samuel almost missed but for God's prompting, Saul got. David was a wonder.

And Saul first wanted to exploit it, and then to destroy it.

Jonathan, Saul's son, also recognized David's greatness. And

Jonathan had more to lose than his father did. Saul was already king. Jonathan was the prince, heir to the throne. David's existence threatened Jonathan's succession. And David excelled at all those things at which Jonathan was good. Music. Leadership. The skill of warfare. The art of wooing.

David was just better.

If Jonathan ever battled his own jealousy and envy toward David, ever nursed a secret ambition to see David fall, he gave no indication of it. Jonathan went in exactly the opposite direction of his father. He became David's biggest champion. He used his considerable power and influence to serve David's cause, because he discerned that it was really God's cause. Paul says that David, after he had served God's purposes for his generation, died (Acts 13:36). That epitaph would be equally fitting for Jonathan: he also served God's purposes in his generation, first by stepping up to help David accomplish God's purposes, and then by stepping back to let David embrace them.

And that's the rub. The question to ask with *the most of these* (in fact, with *all of these*) is simply this: What is God up to here? For what end has God raised up this man or woman, and shown favor to them, and lavished gifts upon them? Discern that, and regardless of whether their success is personally advantageous to you or not, you have discerned the trajectory of your mission: serve God's purposes and then get out of the way.

You might do that, of course, with a clenched jaw. Or you choose to do it with a generous heart. The difference between the two is *agapē*.

BUT *AGAPĒ* CALLS US FURTHER STILL. *AGAPĒ* WOULD HAVE US love, not only the least of these and the most of these, but also *the worst of these.* Your enemy. *The worst of these* is that person you have least reason to like and most reason to hate. It's the person who has betrayed you, hurt you, willfully misunderstood you, taken something precious from you.

We especially need *agapē* here, for it embodies a power in excess of our natural impulse toward hate or fear. It exerts a pull stronger than our hankering for frontier justice, deeper than our lust for vengeance.

Jesus is clear enough about this:

> You have heard that it was said, "Love your neighbor and hate your enemy." But I tell you: Love your enemies and pray for those who persecute you, that you may be sons of your Father in heaven. He causes his sun to rise on the evil and the good, and sends rain on the righteous and the unrighteous. If you love those who love you, what reward will you get? Are not even the tax collectors doing that? And if you greet only your brothers, what are you doing more than others? Do not even pagans do that? Be perfect, therefore, as your heavenly Father is perfect. (Matt. 5:43–48)

Even pagans love those who love them. You don't require supernatural strength to love like that. But to love those whom you have every reason to hate and to hurt—personal reasons, visceral reasons, historical reasons, doctrinal reasons, deep-rooted and long-standing reasons—that takes the Son of God within you.

Gordon is from Canada and his wife, Regine, originally from Rwanda. She survived—barely—the genocide of 1994. She lost many loved ones in that holocaust, those who were easy for her to love: family members, friends. For several months she was a fugitive in her own land. She scavenged, hid in shadows, slept in caves. And she was running, always running.

Finally, she got out. She came to Canada as a refugee. She met Gordon. They fell in love, married. And then—breathtaking, this—they went back to her homeland, Rwanda. She returned, not to take vengeance, but to help others heal. Regine became a Christian during the genocide, when all she had was her sister's Bible. That Bible was bread and water and air to her. Through it, she met Jesus, the *agapē* lover. She met the one who claimed her and healed her by his love, and then gave her, and her husband Gordon, a commission: freely give what you've freely received.

Love as I have loved you.

In a recent letter, her brother, Innocent, summed up just how costly such love is. Innocent is now a schoolteacher in Rwanda. It wasn't long ago these children's parents were wielding clubs and machetes, slaughtering neighbors without mercy. "It's hard," Innocent writes, "to love the children of those who tried to kill you."

But he does. And Regine does. They have discovered a peace and joy in Christ that is not from this world; it overcomes this world. Christ pours into them his *agapē*, and then draws out of them acts of unprovoked love.

Like the story Regine told me one day. Her voice was quiet, light, and musical, as though she was merely recounting a recent family vacation.

A woman's only son was killed. She was consumed with grief and hate and bitterness. "God," she prayed, "reveal my son's killer."

One night she dreamed she was going to heaven. But there was a complication: in order to get to heaven she had to pass through a certain house. She had to walk down the street, enter the house through the front door, go through its rooms, up the stairs, and exit through the back door.

She asked God whose house this was.

It's the house, he told her, of your son's killer.

The road to heaven passed through the house of her enemy.

Two nights later, there was a knock at her door. She opened it, and there stood a young man. He was about her son's age.

"Yes?"

He hesitated. And then he said, "I am the one who killed your son. Since that day, I have had no life. No peace. So here I am. I am placing my life in your hands. Kill me. I am dead already. Throw me in jail. I am in prison already. Torture me. I am in torment already.

"Do with me as you wish."

The woman had prayed for this day. Now it had arrived, and she didn't know what to do. She found, to her own surprise, that she did not want to kill him. Or throw him in jail. Or torture him. In that moment of reckoning, she found she only wanted one thing: a son.

"I ask this of you. Come into my home and live with me. Eat the food I would have prepared for my son. Wear the clothes I would have made for my son. Become the son I lost."

And so he did.

Agapē lovers do what God himself has done, making sons and daughters out of bitter enemies, feeding and clothing them, blazing a trail to heaven straight through their houses. "You see," Paul writes,

> at just the right time, when we were still powerless, Christ died for the ungodly . . . God demonstrates his own love for us in this: While we were still sinners, Christ died for us. . . . When we were God's enemies, we were reconciled to him through the death of his Son. (Rom. 5:6–10)

I SAID THAT *AGAPĒ* IS UNPROVOKED LOVE. THAT'S ONLY HALF true. In God, it is unprovoked. But in us, it is provoked—by God. God sparks it, fuels it, stokes it. "This is love," John says, "not that we loved God, but that *he loved us*" (1 John 4:10; emphasis mine). Paul says: "The love of Christ compels us" (2 Cor. 5:14 NKJV).

There are some ways we will never become *agapē* lovers. We won't get there by trying harder. We won't get there by reading more books. We won't get there by honing up technique. We won't get there by feeding our guilt.

And we certainly won't get there through fear. Indeed, the opposite of *agapē* is not hate, but fear.

> There is no *fear* in love. But perfect love drives out fear, because fear
> has to do with punishment. The one who fears is not made perfect
> in love. (1 John 4:18; emphasis mine)

Fear has to do with judgment. Fear has to do with the sense that I don't measure up. I'm not good enough. I'm not loved. If you knew me, you'd reject me. And when we fear that way, we become evasive and defensive and aggressive. We want to settle scores. We're easily threatened. We're open prey to envy and pride and greed. We try to define ourselves by what we have or what we know or what others think about us. We spend inordinate amounts of time trying to manipulate other people's perception of us.

But the more you realize how high and deep and wide is the love God has for you—yes, *you*—the less you fear.

Love casts it out.

That love—God's *agapē* for you—is the only thing that can provoke *agapē* in us toward the least of these, the most of these, the worst of these.

TRACY IS ONE OF THE WORSHIP LEADERS AT OUR CHURCH. ONE Sunday, as she sat at the piano, she talked about the difficult week she'd just been through. It was chaotic, she said, a mess of petty crises on top of a rash of minor accidents, all mixed up in a soupcon of crazy busyness. It had left her weary and cranky. She got up that Sunday to lead worship and felt spent, with nothing more to give.

She walked into the living room, and the window was covered with scrawl. Her eight-year-old daughter Brenna (I call her Lucy, because of her pitch-perfect resemblance to the character by that name in the movie adaptation of *The Lion, the Witch and the Wardrobe*) had with a glass crayon scribbled something, top to bottom, side to side, across the picture window. At first, it seemed to Tracy one more thing to do, one more mess to clean. Then she saw what Brenna had written: *love, joy, peace, patience, kindnece, goodnece, faithfulnece, gentelnece and selfcantrol* (Brenna's delightful spelling).

Tracy stopped, drank it in. Her heart flooded with light. It was exactly what she needed to be reminded about: the gift of the fruit of the Spirit that arises, not by our circumstances, but by Christ within us.

And then Tracy noticed one more thing Brenna had written, at the edge of the window: *Love one another*. Only, Brenna, in her creative spelling, had written,

Love

won

another. [3]

It's what Jesus has been trying to tell us all along. You were won that way.

Now go and do likewise.

The Petrine Diaries:
Lovesick

"SIMON SON OF JOHN, DO YOU TRULY LOVE ME?"

How odd it must have been for Peter to hear Jesus say those words (see John 21:16). Jesus, a man, with a man's voice, deep-timbered and gravelly. There might well have been occasions when Peter's wife asked him the exact same thing. Maybe she had asked him that, over and over, for the past three years, after he left a perfectly good day job catching fish and took up with that wandering storyteller—a man so broke he had to fetch tax money from fish mouths (Matt. 17:27), scrounge bread and fish from a mere child (John 6:9), pilfer grain from some farmer's field just to feed himself and his followers (Matt. 12), rely on a group of tagalong women to pay the bills (Matt. 27:55).

Peter, how can you do this to me—to us? What am I, chopped liver? That you run off with this . . . this vagabond, this babbler and rambler, with his kooky ideas and made-up stories, and all those floosies who follow him around. I heard one of them even crashed Simon's dinner party and started kissing this man's feet in front of all the guests. It's unseemly, Peter. People are talking. Peter, don't you see? This is crazy! Can't you do one thing for my sake for a change?

Peter, do you truly love me?

Maybe she asked it, variously, in wrath, in heartbreak, in scorn, in resignation.

Who knows. We know nothing about Mrs. Peter the Apostle, except that she existed (Luke 4:38; 1 Cor. 9:5), and that she was among those whom Peter apparently left in order to follow Jesus (Luke 18:28–29).

But did she not once look at her man, angry or quizzical, sad or hurt, and ask, *Peter, do you love me?*

I'd be surprised if she didn't.

They must have been young once. They must have known that season of courtship when each couldn't wait to see the other, where just the thought of the other's voice or smile was like knowing a secret passageway in an old house. There must have been times when, sitting in synagogue while the old rabbi droned on, they kept stealing glances across the rows, until their mothers *tchhed* at them, goaded them with an elbow, told them to pay attention. There must have been those first days and weeks of marriage, when Peter rushed home each day after work, the older men laughing at him, just to touch again her soft slender nakedness, hear her say his name whisperingly.

Do you love me, Peter?

But by the time we meet up with Peter in the Gospels—running, hauling, boasting, quarreling, flailing swords, fleeing courtyards—his wife, his nameless wife, is a mere rumor. When Peter was not disastrously double-minded, he was frighteningly single-minded. He could not, it seems, love two things at once, both Jesus and her.

And yet we have small hints that this changed, that his love for Jesus widened and deepened to reawaken, to reignite, his love for her. We have subtle clues that Peter's devotion to Jesus, rather than displacing all other devotions, in time purified and perfected them. Maybe Peter only really, truly loved his wife after he grasped the height and width and depth of what it meant to love Jesus and have Jesus love him.

"Peter, do you truly love me?"

Then feed my sheep.

Which includes Greta (or Betty, or Mildred, or Naomi, whatever his wife's name was).

What hints do we have for this? Well, for one, Paul's comment in 1 Corinthians:

> Don't we have the right to take a believing wife along with us, as do the other apostles and the Lord's brothers *and Cephas*? (1 Cor. 9:5; emphasis mine). Note: Cephas is yet another name for Peter.

She became an integral part of Peter's life and ministry. Peter discovered that Jesus's love is not some narrow, rigid thing. It is wide and deep and wild, loosing on earth what it looses in heaven. It is passionate and tender and resilient. Devotion to Christ does not cancel out devotion to others, but completes it. Peter learned to do what Paul later told all husbands to do—to love his wife as Christ loved the church, giving himself up for her (Eph. 5:25ff). He learned what others make plain—that if he loves the church and not his wife, feeds all the sheep but not his own, he has "denied the faith and is worse than an unbeliever" (1 Tim. 5:8).

That's one hint that Peter renewed his love for his wife.

The other is in something Peter himself writes, in his first letter.

> Husbands, in the same way be considerate as you live with your wives, and treat them with respect as the weaker partner and as heirs with you of the gracious gift of life, so that nothing will hinder your prayers. (1 Pet. 3:7)

It would be an act of brazen hypocrisy for any man to write this who wasn't also living it. If Peter commends to us attitudes and actions that he himself ignores, he falls under his own condemnation, his fierce rejection of those who "mouth empty, boastful words" and "promise . . . freedom, while they themselves are slaves" (2 Pet. 2:18–19).

But I think it was otherwise. I think Peter became an example of uxorious devotion, of husbandly affection. I think that in the matter of loving his wife he could say, as Paul said elsewhere, "Join with others in following my example, brothers. . . . Whatever you have learned or received or heard from me, or seen in me—put it into practice. And the God of peace will be with you" (Phil. 3:17, 4:9).

I think Peter discovered that the love of Christ frees us to love, not only the least of these and most of these and worst of these, but also and just as much the most-taken-for-granted of these. Who are often our own children. Our own spouse.

In Christ, love comes full circle. It not only reaches heaven's glories, stoops to Sheol's blackness, extends to the outermost ends of the earth. It also turns the heart toward home, so that the wife of your youth becomes the queen of your days and the love of your life.

And only then do our prayers get heard.

The Wife's Tale

He came back to me after I'd stopped waiting. You understand, yes, that a woman who waits and a woman who gave up waiting are not the same woman, not at all. My heart was wood and stone. My heart was bitter root and dry husk. My heart's last gate closed, and I locked it. And only then did he come back.

I did not want him. I could not abide his big, thick body leaving its stains and smells and molting in every inch and corner. His heaviness hollowed out the places he laid. I'd find his debris everywhere: mud from the seashore left on my kitchen floor, hair from his back-thatch littered across my bed, hair from his grizzled beard coiled wet inside my wash basin like an arabesque of cracks, scales from the fish he went back to catching flecking all he'd brush against. I once found these things a comfort, mementoes of his presence, harbingers of his return. But not now. Now they are to me only work, intrusion, omen.

I didn't understand how Jesus could do this to us: pull our lives apart. We once were happy, in a reasonable way. We had a life. He had a job. Not a lot of money, but we made do. We were tired most of the time (what couple is not?) and didn't talk much (what couple does?) and our love life was nothing to speak of (what couple's is?). But we got by.

And then Jesus. He came and called Peter, and Peter never even asked me. He just decided. He was like that. But Jesus should have known that about him. Jesus should have asked Peter to think it over awhile, to weigh it out, to talk to his wife about these things. We might have reached a compromise. I'd spent our entire marriage compensating for that man, being shrewd to protect from his naiveté, being cautious to make up for his rashness, being suspicious because he was overly trusting, being stingy, just a bit, or else he'd have squandered what little we had. I went slow at things because he ran reckless, and usually stumbled.

And then Jesus broke all that asunder.

I was angry enough to die. I thought of a thousand things to do, to take revenge, to take control, but did none. Peter stayed away longer and longer, and I got so I liked it. I found other things to do. I found ways to survive. The house became very quiet. In the late afternoons I would sit where sunlight fell into the room, large squares of it that grew narrow and sharp as they shuttled up the wall, until they were gone altogether and the room was a cool cupful of shadow.

For the first time, I felt still.

Then one day, Peter didn't come home at all. I heard rumors about his whereabouts. They were heading to Jerusalem. There was going to be a war there, or something. I didn't know what to believe. After a time, I didn't care.

My hurt had turned to bitterness, and then withered into apathy. I was content with my emptiness. I was alone, and it was good.

And then he came back.

That was a long time ago now. I still don't grasp all of it, is the truth. We had, after we started talking again, many conversations—Peter trying to explain, me trying to understand, but always we missed each other.

What changed it all was him. It took me months to see this, but the man who returned was not the man who had left. The man who came in the door had a strange and quiet courage about him, the courage of a man who had already died and so found little on this earth to frighten him. And he listened now, his big head bent down and his wide, thick brow creased with thought.

But mostly, he prayed. He reached out his large, rough hands—hands that softened a little each week after he stopped fishing—and folded my hands into his, gentle as though he were gathering something fragile, something he was being careful not to damage, and he prayed. He asked God, with a childlikeness that made me both want to laugh and cry, to come near to us, and often I'm sure I felt something brush the skin just where my neck touched my hair. Peter prayed for food and shelter, for the church, for those who suffered for their faith, for those who as yet did not trust Jesus. He prayed for more faith, a prayer he prayed like breathing.

And he prayed for us.

His words were like that sunlight that fell into that room, and I felt that same stillness I felt before.

Only, this was better.

And one day, I understood: this was the man I had been waiting for all my life.

III

Reap a Harvest

12

Peter's Funny Math

WE'VE TAKEN A LONG JOURNEY ON WHAT AT FIRST LOOKED LIKE
meager provisions, a mere seven verses. It turns out we had more
than enough. We've basketfuls left over. Peter, chatterbox Peter,
proved in the end a knack for conciseness. It's taken me nore than
fifty-thousand words to comment on his few, and still I've barely
started.

But we must make an end of it.

Before we do, though, it's worthwhile to remember what Peter
claimed for these seven virtues:

> For if you possess these qualities in increasing measure, they will
> keep you from being ineffective and unproductive in your knowl-
> edge of our Lord Jesus Christ. But if anyone does not have them, he
> is nearsighted and blind, and has forgotten that he has been
> cleansed from his past sins. (2 Pet. 1:8–9)

You will thrive if you take hold of them, and languish if you
don't. Possess them in increasing measure, and the life of Christ can
flow unimpeded through you. But fail to acquire them, and you'll

end up like that old cartoon character, Mr. Magoo, nearsighted, absentminded, swerving every which way, wreaking havoc to which mostly you're oblivious. All that, and worse: you'll forget you've been forgiven, and so live like you're not.

Until I took that seriously, it hadn't occurred to me that my seasons of stuckness were owing to undernourished virtue. I thought the main cause lay elsewhere—the devil's devices, life's pressures, the season I was in. It was someone or something else's fault. I had a rotating gallery of those I could blame. Whenever I fell into old ways of thinking and behaving, whenever I became ineffective and unproductive in my knowledge of Jesus, I could go off on a blistering tirade about who or what sabotaged me. *If only*, was a favorite refrain. *If only people would listen. If only someone would help. If only we had more time or money. Then I might make some headway.*

Stuckness has nothing to with any of that. It has, almost always, to do with me. Peter helped me see that. I already have everything I need for life and godliness. I can, today, participate in the divine nature and escape the corruption of the world. I can be thick as thieves in the things of God, cagey as Houdini with the wiles of the evil one. God can't get rid of me and the world can't catch me.

That life has been made available to me in full.

Only, there's some assembly required. Now I must make every effort to attain what I already possess—or, more to the point, to fully possess what I've already attained. A car never driven goes nowhere. A dollar never spent buys nothing. An *I love you* never spoken woos no one. I can gain the whole world, and heaven besides, but lose it simply by not using it. I can let supernatural provision, like manna, molder from stockpiling.

Peter tells me I have gained the whole world, and heaven besides. And he tells me therefore to do what at first blush seems counter-intuitive but, once pondered, makes the only sense: *make every effort.* Get to work. Dig and stretch and reach and struggle. Throw yourself headlong and two-fisted into the fray. Make it all count.

We've studied these seven verses at book-length. Peter, in the two verses right after these seven, ups the ante even higher—all the way to the threshold of the pearly gates where, legend has it, he now sits.

> Therefore, my brothers, be all the more eager to make your calling and election sure. For if you do these things, you will never fall, and you will receive a rich welcome into the eternal kingdom of our Lord and Savior Jesus Christ. (2 Pet. 1:10–11)

These seven virtues—goodness, knowledge, self-control, perseverance, godliness, brotherly kindness, love—are touchstones of election and calling. They are our primary evidence that God in Christ has chosen us and spoken to us. More than that, Peter indicates that our election and calling, vouched for by these virtues, guarantees a life that is unassailable on earth and richly rewarded in heaven.

We won't fall and we can't lose.

> So I will always remind you of these things, *even though you know them and are firmly established in the truth you now have.* (2 Pet. 1:12; emphasis mine)

We already know all this.
But it's good to get a reminder.

THE DAY OUR SON ADAM CAME INTO THE WORLD I DROVE THE long way home, down a bending narrow country lane. It was early spring and early morning. Sunlight, pale but sharp, entwined with tree shadows, thin as smoke, and together danced across my windshield. The car's interior had a lovely coolness to it, like a garden at dawn, and this helped me stay alert.

Adam's our firstborn. Your firstborn redefines everything, the whole wide world, just by showing up. So I had a lot to think about. My wife had had a long, bitter labor, thirty-six grueling hours of it followed by an emergency C-section, and in the course of that day half my existence underwent seismic upheaval. I was now a father. And I was the father of a *son*—both my wife and I, by that voodoo logic that sometimes mesmerizes expecting couples, had thoroughly convinced ourselves it was a girl pushing her midriff into a taut bulge: a delicate, porcelain doll of a daughter, cooing and blinking, lover of cats and lace.

We were wrong. It was a boy, a husky, ruddy lad who could howl maniacally, pull the house apart with his bare hands, clog toilets with innovative combinations of tissue wads and toy cars, rip pages from books just to hear the sound of them rending. We couldn't have been more surprised than if she'd given birth to a platypus.

Not that we were disappointed.

Just surprised.

So I had a lot to think about. For nine months, or thereabouts— ever since that morning that a beaker of my wife's bodily fluid had stained a little pill blue and she announced she was with child—I had subtly but powerfully imagined life with a girl. I would gather her on my lap after a bath and, with surgical gentleness, brush her hair, stroke after stroke until her heavy damp tresses, from crown to shoulder, lay together flat and neat and straight like the edges of pages in a closed book. I would read her stories of ponies and puppies. We would shop together for her mother's birthday, looking at turtlenecks and bracelets and slippers with furry lining. At night, I'd tuck her into bed, her and her stuffy, and kiss her on the forehead gently as a butterfly lighting there.

Nine months of such imagining, cliché as it is, takes powerful hold of a man. (Later, I did have a girl, and then another, and discovered soon enough that my notions of both chivalry and femininity were mostly ill-advised.)

But for now I had a boy, and had no idea what to do next. I'd failed to prepare. I had not conjured even a single picture of how a male child would alter my life differently from a female child—would require, in some matters, a different kind of parent. On that drive home, that conjuring happened in earnest. My son's advent awakened in me things long dormant. Tricks with knives. Stunts on bikes. Uses of chainsaws. The secrets and dangers of fire. How to hide fear in a showdown. How to spool out a loop of fly line at your feet and cast it, slow and smooth, until you set it down on the water as quietly as you'd lay a sleeping child.

I pictured the two of us repairing a bike tube—I'd show him how to use a crescent wrench and loosen the bolts and wiggle the wheel out of the forks and pry the tire's lip up over the wheel's chrome rim and tease out the deflated tube, and how to overfill the tube with air and dredge it through a tub of water until you saw a thin geyser of bubbles streaming from an otherwise invisible hole, and how to mark that hole and score it rough and brush it with a thin sheen of glue and press and hold the patch to it, and then how to set the entire procedure in reverse.

I'd show him how to use a cross blade and a mitre saw, an edge plane and T-bevel, and how to laminate wood so that it doesn't warp on you. We would camp together, and make fires from brushwood, and cook fresh-caught trout in sweet grass and butter.

It was an alpha-male fantasy all the way, I see that now, but most of it we've, in fact, done. Not long ago, before the snows came, Adam and I took our bikes up the ski mountain near to where we live, took the lift to the top, and rode the bikes down over stone fields and grassy tussocks, through reedy swales and swampy bogs. We arrived at the bottom sheathed in mud, drenched to the skin, with bruises already blooming from our many falls.

And so alive.

I'M TELLING YOU ALL THIS TO ILLUSTRATE A VERY SIMPLE point: what we imagine matters. The future we picture shapes the reality we create, for good or ill.

This book has been an attempt to help you imagine a future different, perhaps, from the one you've been living toward. It's to remind you that something utterly good, beyond what you asked or imagined, has come into your life through Christ, but that to taste the fullness of this gift you must embrace it with passion and imagination and discipline.

You must make every effort.

God's already given you everything you need for the life you've always dreamed—a life where you have, in abundance, the kindness that allows you to overlook and overcome an insult; have, in spades, the knowledge that makes you deeply effective and highly productive; have, in excess, the self-control that empowers you to take off lust, anger, envy, and put on peace, love, generosity. All of these things flourish already in your life, right at hand, close enough for you to gather in fistfuls and armloads.

But you have to make the effort.

There is a strange calculus in Peter's seven virtues. Peter begins simply enough, employing the rudiments of arithmetic: add this to that, he says. Take this one thing, and join it to this next thing, and then another, and another. Repeat the process from the beginning. It all has a grade-school simplicity to it. It's no more complicated, and at times almost as tedious, as writing a single line a hundred times on a chalkboard: *I will not dunk Peggy Sue's pigtail in the ink pot . . .*

But the consequences are stunning. This rudimentary arithmetic results in geometric, exponential growth: simple addition tips at some point and becomes runaway multiplication. Splice together ordinary virtues, a little goodness to a bit of self-control, add a pinch of godliness, repeat and repeat, and one day the combination shoots through the roof. You find yourself God-like in strength, Christlike in attitude.

Just from adding things up.

IN *THE FELLOWSHIP OF THE RING*, THE FIRST MOVIE OF THE Lord of the Rings, Frodo and Sam are leaving their beloved shire, a land of streams and valleys and meadows and forests. They are on a journey that will take them to the very ends of the earth, only they don't know that yet. They think they're simply traveling to the next county.

As they cross a field, Sam stops. Frodo stops as well.

"What's the matter, Sam?"

"If I take one more step," Sam says, "I'll have gone further than I've been before."

Frodo smiles, walks back to him, puts his arm around him,

"Come on, Sam. As Gandalf says, it's a dangerous thing, just going out your door."

And, together, they take the next step, and the next, and the next, into dangers and wonders beyond imagining, into a life that transforms them both. Into life to the full.

They *really* lived.

Why don't you take a step further than you've ever gone before, and see where the road goes?

13

A Year with Peter

THIS PAST YEAR, I'VE MADE A TRAVELING COMPANION OF PETER.

I've always loved Paul, though at times he leaves me gasping to catch up. I've always loved David, though at times he ventures places I know I best not follow. But until this year, until this book, I never walked much with Peter. He was a man I visited now and then, like a deacon, or an uncle from another town. He was someone I was related to in some tenuous way, had some vague and complicated obligations toward, but whose company I rarely sought. Likely, as I said somewhere in this book, it was because I felt an uncomfortable affinity with him, with the flaws in him that reminded me altogether too much of myself.

Now I've spent a year alongside Peter, and I wish I'd started earlier.

Peter's greatest strength, I've come to believe, is one he doesn't even mention in his sevenfold list of virtues, though he speaks of it elsewhere: humility.[1] I had for years noticed Peter's surface, his swagger and boasting, but missed his depths. Deep down, he had simplicity of heart. He had humility. One evidence for this is that the early Christians told and retold stories about Peter, stories in which he rarely appeared wise and poised but instead foolish and weak, easily frightened. Peter, through Mark, was the source of many of these stories. He lets us see the man he was—sinking in water, flailing with sword, falling asleep at the prayer meeting, sputtering nonsense, denying his dearest friend.

In the end, the narration of his many failures makes him easier to trust. That's the irony of humility: the more a man admits his failings, the more likely we are to throw in our lot with him. There is no fool so dangerous as an unknowing fool. But a fool who can confess it, and learn from it, is the fool we trust, for he's learning wisdom. We might go to the ends of the earth with someone like that.

So I'm learning from Peter the power of genuine humility—of not being afraid of how others see me, so long as I'm assured that Jesus sees me, and knows me, and forgives me—and, always, that he loves me. For Peter, Christ's opinion of him mattered more than anyone else's, including his own. That's a key to humility: Christ is first and last, his word the final authority, and if he says I am a new creation, I am, even against evidence that says otherwise. Humility is when Jesus's verdict on everything—me, you, God, the world—annuls my own, regardless of how strongly mine is felt.

I'M ALSO LEARNING FROM PETER THE ART OF LEADING FROM behind. This was not a natural position for him, or for me. Despite what I just said about Peter's humility, the man loved the forefront. He loved the helm, even if he didn't know which direction to take once he got there. But some impulse in him, part child, part bully, part curiosity-hound, part daredevil, kept thrusting him to the front of the pack.

It almost always got him in trouble.

Yet Jesus never rebuked Peter for his desire to lead. Jesus never scolded him for it. He just showed him that being first and greatest comes from the back of the line. Jesus taught him, by example mostly, that leadership and servanthood are in fact the same, that to practice one is to do the other. Touching lepers, washing feet, feeding ragamuffins, being obedient even unto death—these are not merely pathways to leadership: they are its fullest embodiment. Servanthood is the way greatness signs its name.

So Peter, who once rebuked Jesus for trooping toward a cross, and another time for stooping to wash feet, himself learned to go and do likewise. The tradition is that Peter, about to be killed in the same manner Jesus was, asked to be crucified upside-down. His captors were delighted to comply—it added to the carnivalesque atmosphere, the bawdiness and luridness of the spectacle. But Peter was thinking of something else: he did not consider himself to be worthy of a death that mirrored his Savior's. His death would be like Jesus's death, but also unlike it. It would be both a mimicry and a parody of it.[2]

Our leadership and servanthood is that way too: both mimicry and parody of Jesus's own. We mimic his, and yet our imitation is never anything more than a rough facsimile of it, a kind of upside-down pantomime. It's a tribute, for sure, but with a hint of slapstick.

It's near impossible for us to do otherwise. It's hard not to be a little self-conscious about our own virtue. It's hard not to grand-stand our acts of humble service. Jesus, for instance, washed his disciples' feet in an act of pure humility. I doubt, ever since, any-one has ever washed another's feet without at least a shadow of pride in their humility, a twinge of self-congratulations for their willingness to stoop so low. Or this: Jesus welcomed the least of these with unfeigned grace. I'm guessing, ever since, rare have been the moments when one of his followers has done the same without at least an afterthought of calculation, a hidden hope that great will be their reward. Mimicry and parody are all bound up together for us. We approximate an imitation, but it's always a tad askew, sometimes entirely upside-down.

Peter, by my reckoning, got as close as anyone to truly leading from behind. More and more we see him stooping to conquer, becoming great by becoming small, gaining the world by forsaking it, saving his life by losing it. More and more, his mimicry of Jesus loses its self-conscious edge, becomes second nature. More and more, he imitates Christ, not as technique, but as instinct.

The only way from here to there is a "long obedience in the same direction."[3] It's by making our acts intentional until they become habitual and instinctual. It's to practice servant leadership through all those seasons when it seems awkward and contrived, a bit of fakery and puffery for the sake of appearances, but doing it until it is genuine. One day we cross a line, the divide between appearance and essence, and what we do is who we are, true servant leaders.

ONE MORE THING I'M LEARNING FROM PETER: HOW TO WORK fruitfully with those different from myself. The relationship between Peter and Paul was, by all appearances, wary and prickly for a long time. These men were oil and water: Paul stern, resolute, scholarly; Peter companionable, wishy-washy, folksy. Paul came to Christ in a showdown, in a sudden and stark revelation; Peter on a road trip, through a slow and gentle unveiling. Paul was accosted, Peter coaxed.

And this suited them both. It honored who each of them was.

But their relationship with each other got off to a rough start.

A freshly converted Paul shows up at the Apostles' Club in Jerusalem, and Peter wants nothing to do with him. Paul is hardly the humble penitent. He is no prodigal returning, ready to grovel for bread, to offer himself, in rags and tears, as a farmhand or an errand boy. He claims apostleship. Having only recently left a disciple-maiming ministry, he now claims to be in a disciple-making one. This sudden turnabout feels a little off to the other apostles. If not for Barnabas, a powerful influence among them, Paul might well have been stonewalled, left to languish in obscurity. Even still, it's not long before Peter and the apostles send Paul packing off to Antioch. It seems almost a dodge on their part, a maneuver to distance themselves from him. But Paul is irrepressible, and soon he's evangelizing the Gentile world so aggressively that it causes deep controversy back in Jerusalem and leads to the first theological council in history (Acts 15).

Later, Paul comes back and publicly dresses down Peter for shilly-shallying on his relationships with Gentiles. Peter, the force behind overturning Jewish laws of diet and Jewish customs of interracial association within the early church, had lapsed, under pressure, into his old exclusivism, his ancient practice of apartheid. To Paul, this was sheer hypocrisy—and he said so, to Peter's face, with others watching (Gal. 2:11, 14).

None of this could have done much to endear each to the other.

But at some point, these two titans had to come together. For sake of the gospel, in obedience to the one they followed, it had to be done.

I wonder if, for Peter, it might have started with that public rebuke. Did it remind him of another rebuke, long ago, from the lips of someone else: "Get behind, me, Satan! . . . You do not have in mind the things of God but the things of men" (Matt. 16:23)? We don't know. What we do know is that Peter, near the end of his old life, called Paul "our dear brother," and commended him for "the wisdom that God gave him" (2 Pet. 3:15). And then Peter wrote this about Paul's writings:

> His letters contain some things that are hard to understand, which ignorant and unstable people distort, as they do the other Scriptures, to their own destruction. (2 Pet. 3:16)

I think this is remarkable. At a point where Peter, even subtly, might have taken a swipe at Paul, might just have winked a bit at his readers, he refuses. Paul has become to him a dear brother, replete with heaven-borne wisdom, and if others don't understand him, that's their problem, not Paul's.

In my life I have worked with many people quite different from me and haven't always handled it well. I've found it easy to perceive others' differences as flaws and vices. The degree others didn't agree with me, the script went, is the degree to which they were flat-out wrong. There's been a tendency in me to take refuge in petty distinctions: I've kept my own little glossary of shibboleths, and if you didn't pronounce them just the way I did, it meant you had an impediment.

If Peter had a tendency like that once, and I think he did, he overcame it. He made every effort to add virtue to his faith—things such as goodness, knowledge, self-control, perseverance, godliness. He added brotherly kindness. He added love.

And so he became a man who turned former enemies and potential rivals into dear brothers.

If ever the church needed men like that again, it's now.

The Brother's Tale

Always I admired him, even when I could scarcely abide him. Truth: everything about my brother was thick. Thick skin, thick hair, thick bones, thick tongue, thick skull. It was astonishing to see him on open water when the fish were running, this thick man turned nimble as a cat. Every sinew in him bent to the task, and for that instant all his thickness became litheness. But if he was just sitting, staring at the water as he often did, he was dense as a boulder, a monument of immovable heft. I sometimes got so angry at him, angry at his thickness, I wanted to hit his big brambly head with wood or rock. But then he would do something, something brave or foolish, or both, and I felt ashamed for thinking such thoughts.

When we were boys we shared a room. At night, Simon showed me how to make shapes on the walls with shadows from my hands. He showed me how to hold my hands close to the lantern, where the light was sharpest, and twist or stretch them, curl them into balls or splay them into pinwheels, so that roosters strutted and wolves stalked and snakes slithered across the uneven surface of our back wall. He made me laugh, because he'd tell stories to go along with our pantomime of shades, and he talked in the voices of the creatures we were portraying: the wolf's voice nasally and menacing, the rooster's thin-throated and haughty, the snake's lisping and soothing, the lion's deep and slow. Afterward, when the lantern was out and the room was unearthly dark, I listened to Peter sleeping—he breathed heavy even then, soughing and blowing—and I would carry on the stories in my head, finish them, refashion them. Give them happy endings.

Of course, we outgrew that. Peter became more serious as he got older. He carried unseen things, a swelling weight of them. My father was often angry, and he took most of that out on Simon. *Simon, what is this mess? Simon, what were you thinking? Simon, I said* now! I watched my brother grow stern and brusque and deliberate beneath my father's mindless harangues, and more and more I watched my brother mimic him.

But always I admired him, even when I could scarcely abide him.

John the Baptist introduced me to Jesus. That's a whole story altogether. I had become a disciple of John's. Simon never knew what to make of John, and that was maybe part of my motivation for following him. I don't know myself. I think I wanted, just once, to do something Simon wasn't doing, to find something he hadn't found first. To cast my own shadow. To find my own voice. John was half-crazy, we all saw that: he dressed like a beggar, and hollered like a madman, and ate things that stained his teeth and left his breath reeking foul. Simon never would say anything outright bad about him, but he didn't pay him much heed, either. I think he found John too much like our father, always yelling. And Simon never had time for people who had no steady work, work they might hate but they did every day anyhow.

John was a hard master, is the truth. We never knew him. His eyes bespoke vast depths, but undisclosed. Some hidden compass guided the man, some tug and prod from within or beyond, and he would do things and say things that startled us in their utter strangeness. He took us by surprise, always.

Like the day Jesus walked by. I was with John, and another of his disciples, and Jesus strolled past. John said, "Look, the Lamb of God."

And that was enough. Everything became instantly clear. I looked, saw Jesus, and then he was all I saw. John's other disciple and I broke into a run to catch up with him. I knew he could hear us coming from a distance—we were as loud as cart horses—but he kept walking at a steady pace, neither hastening nor slowing. His back was a mute invitation, and in my mind I saw him smiling, amused and pleased. Then when we were virtually skinning his heels, and panting hard, he turned around—I see that still, the casualness of it, his head pivoting like a weather vane and his feet not missing a step—and he simply asked, "What do you want?"

"Rabbi," we both said, "where are you staying?"

It seems stupid to me now, the question. *Where are you staying?* It was so abrupt, presumptuous, intrusive.

But he treated the question as though we had uttered the wisdom of Solomon. "Come, and you will see." We went with him, and spent the day talking, questioning, listening.

And we never were the same again.

The first person I wanted to tell was Simon. "Simon, we found him!"

"Found who?"

"The Messiah. The Christ."

"Andrew, this isn't another one of your shaggy wild men with bad teeth, is it?"

"Simon, you've got to come and see. This is the one John told us about. He's the real thing, Peter. Please, come and see."

And so he did. And Jesus, when he saw my brother, said, "You are Simon, son of John. You will be called Peter."

And just the way he said it, there was no gainsaying. Peter believed at that instant. He never looked back.

But I did, a few times. Not that I ever doubted Jesus. I just felt useless, and sometimes used. Peter quickly became Jesus's closest friend, and so did our fishing partners, James and John. And I was left on the outside. Me, the one there first. I was typically sent to fetch bread for dinner, while those three toddled off on another private excursion with Jesus, to be told exquisite secrets for their ears only, shown dazzling epiphanies for their eyes alone. Jesus swore them not to tell the rest of us, not right away, but they always managed to let us know that they knew something we didn't. I watched them leave, comrades, coconspirators, laughing over their inside jokes, while I and the others were left to break camp or scour pots, and I felt a sourness that took me days to shake. I watched them return, solemn with new understanding, stiffly proud with secrecy, and bitterness would overcome me.

Peter was oblivious. He just enjoyed his status, sometimes wielded it like my father might have, and never noticed that I was the errand boy. I watched him sitting by the fire at night, his body casting a huge shadow, a caricature of himself that lumbered and reeled on the rocks behind us, and I wanted to hit him square across that big thick head of his, hit him hard for his thickness.

But then something changed. In him. In me. He became less and less like my father and more and more like Jesus. And me? I discovered that being like John the Baptist, pointing others to Jesus so that they could follow—well, who wants more than that?

Call me Peter's brother.

CROSSINGS®

THE BOOK CLUB FOR TODAY'S CHRISTIAN FAMILY

A Letter to Our Readers

Dear Reader:

In order that we might better contribute to your reading enjoyment, we would appreciate your taking a few minutes to respond to the following questions. When completed, please return to the following:

Andrea Doering, Editor-in-Chief
Crossings Book Club
401 Franklin Avenue, Garden City, NY 11530

You can post your review online! Go to www.crossings.com and rate this book.

Title _____ Author _____

1   Did you enjoy reading this book?

❑ Very much. I would like to see more books by this author!

❑ I really liked_____

❑ Moderately. I would have enjoyed it more if_____

2   What influenced your decision to purchase this book? Check all that apply.

      ❑ Cover
      ❑ Title
      ❑ Publicity
      ❑ Catalog description
      ❑ Friends
      ❑ Enjoyed other books by this author
      ❑ Other _____

3   Please check your age range:

      ❑ Under 18   ❑ 18-24
      ❑ 25-34   ❑ 35-45
      ❑ 46-55   ❑ Over 55

4   How many hours per week do you read? _____

5   How would you rate this book, on a scale from 1 (poor) to 5 (superior)?

_____

Name_____

Occupation_____

Address_____

City_____ State_____ Zip_____

Acknowledgments

Writing books, I'm finding, gets no easier with each new one. This is my fifth, and it wrung from me just as much sweat and time as each of the previous four. First you quarry, next you sculpt, and then you polish, and all are hard and bruising tasks. It is both a relief and a sorrow to be done.

There are many people to thank this side of things. Several good (and honest) friends—Jeremy Bell, Joy Brewtser, Greg Daniel, Rob Filgate, Ann Spangler—read through an earlier draft and both encouraged me and pushed me to do better. Bless you. This book's virtues, whatever they may be, are greater for your efforts. Kate Etue and Recah Theodosiou edited the whole book with breathtaking swiftness but no loss of agility.

My publisher, Greg Daniel, has not only done his job with excellence but has been a companion in the journey. My agent, Ann Spangler, also. Rob Filgate and Allan Kinnee continue to be brothers-in-arms. Your friendship is bracing and refreshing like the rivers we swim in together.

Cheryl, my wife of now more than twenty years, is my Shulamite beauty. This year, through the writing of this book, we walked together through one of the hardest seasons of our life—the slow, messy death of my dear colleague and her best friend, Carol Boschma (to whom I've dedicated this work). Cheryl, your courage, compassion, and strength throughout has filled me with even greater thankfulness for you. I love you.

My children—my, how they grow—continue to delight me and give me touchstones of what is real and true and good. I love you.

Our church, New Life Community Baptist, pastors me as much as I do it. You are a remarkable company of people to abide with. It is no chore to get up each morning and discover with you treasures that God has hidden in plain sight.

Mostly, I thank God for his Son, Jesus, and Jesus for sending his Spirit. Each year I seek and savor your presence more. All glory is yours. Amen and amen.

Shalom,

MARK BUCHANAN
August 2006
Duncan, British Columbia

Notes

Chapter 1

1. Daniel Boorstin, *Hidden History: Exploring Our Secret Past* (New York: Harper & Row, 1987), 171-172.
2. Mark Buchanan, *Your God is Too Safe* (Sisters, OR: Multnomah, 2001).
3. Edmund Spenser, *The Faerie Queene*, bk. 1, canto 4.
4. The medieval church also formulated four cardinal virtues-prudence, temperance, justice & fortitude-and three theological virtues-faith, hope and love. The difference between them: cardinal virtues can be cultivated; theological virtues only received.

Chapter 2—Faith, part 1

1. *Ray*, Universal Studios, 2004; starring Jamie Foxx.
2. Vernon Grounds, *Our Daily Bread*, "Apatheists," Monday, June 21, 2004.
3. Paul Adams, "Faith," *Leadership Journal* (Summer 1992), 47.

Chapter 3—Faith, part 2

1. Warren Bennis, *On Becoming a Leader* (New York: Adisson-Wesley, 1989), 195.
2. Martin Luther, Letter 99, Paragraph 13 in *Dr. Martin Luther's Saemmtliche Schriften*, Vol. 15, ed. Dr. Johann Georg Walch, trans. Erika Bullmann Flores (St. Louis: Concordia, date unknown), 2585-2590.
3. Martin Luther, *The Collected Works of Martin Luther*, Vol. 24, quoted in Martin Luther, *Faith Alone: A Daily Devotional*, ed. James C. Galvin (Grand Rapids: Zondervan, 2005), Feb. 21 entry.
4. Ibid., April 18 entry.
5. Pat Conroy, *The Prince of Tides* (New York: The Dial Press, 2005), 90.

Chapter 5—Goodness

1. Harold J. Sala, *Heroes* (Promise, 1998); Cited in *Leadership Journal*, Fall 2000, 71.
2. *MacLean's Magazine*, date & issue unknown.
3. R.W.D., "Are You For Real?" *Our Daily Bread*, June 11, 1988.

Chapter 6—Knowledge

1. Bill Bryson, *A Short History of Nearly Everything* (Toronto: Doubleday Canada, 2003), 6.

Chapter 7—Self-Control

1. Jack Groppel, "The Mental Toughness of a Leader," address at *Willow Creek Leadership* Summit, August 12, 2005.
2. C. S. Lewis, *The Lion, the Witch & the Wardrobe* (Middlesex, England: Puffin Books, 1978), 148.
3. Galatians 2:11ff

Chapter 8—Perseverance

1. Source unknown.
2. Michael P. Green, ed., *Illustrations for Biblical Preaching* (Grand Rapids: Baker Book House, 1991), 264.
3. *Rabbit-Proof Fence* (Mirimax Home Entertainment, 2002).
4. The phrase is from A. J. Conyer, *The Eclipse of Heaven* (Intervarsity Press, 1992), 67.
5. Barbara Amiel, "A timeless hero for troubled times," *MacLean's*, September 25, 1995, 9.

Chapter 11—Love

1. A. J. Conyer, *The Eclipse of Heaven* (Intervarsity Press, 1992), 185
2. Rabbi Paysach Krohn, *Echoes of the Maggid* (Artscroll, 1999), page unknown.
3. Tracy Bazinet, told at New Life Community Baptist Church, May 21, 2006; used by permission.
4. See 1 Peter 5:6 for Peter's famous call to humility.
5. The manner of Peter's death is described by Eusebius (*Ecclesiastical History* 2.25.5-8). St. Jerome mentions the tradition that this was Peter's request.
6. The quote is originally from F. Nietzsche, but Eugene Peterson used it for a title of one of his books.